LOCOMOTIVES
in detail

MAUNSELL 4-6-0 8 **LORD NELSON CLASS**

LOCOMOTIVES
in detail
8

MAUNSELL 4-6-0   **LORD NELSON CLASS**

PETER SWIFT

Ian Allan
PUBLISHING

Acknowledgements

This is the fourth in this series of books to deal with locomotives of the Southern Railway and completes the trilogy on the express locomotives of R.E.L.Maunsell. The 'Lord Nelson' class always held a special place in my affections. During the time when I was living in Winchester, between 1947 and 1962, all were running on the Waterloo to Bournemouth main line. From my usual train watching spot by St Cross signalbox, the 'Nelsons' became the only class of locomotive of which I was aware of having seen all of them. I was never a very serious 'spotter'; watching the trains go past being more my line than following up missing numbers.

Many years later, the 'Nelson' is the only class of locomotive of which I have a 'full house' in my 4mm scale model collection. The 16 models represent one of each locomotive at various periods during the life of the class and, including livery variants, are all different. This was not achieved by high-quality modelling, all but one being modified from the Bachmann model and do not claim to contain every correct detail. No.851 was built some years earlier from a brass and whitemetal kit. Why No.851? – an examination of the parts of the kit showed that No.851, in post 1939 condition, was the only 'Nelson' which could be built from the kit with no alterations! The purpose of this book is to provide modellers with information on the changes which occurred to the external appearance of the 'Lord Nelson' class over the years.

Numerous books and articles have been published describing various aspects of the locomotives, those which have been of most use in preparing the text for this book are listed in the bibliography, in the order of publication. In his *Book of the Lord Nelsons*, Richard Derry comments on the non-availability of official documentation on the class. At the time he was researching for his book, the Engine Record Cards for the class were with amongst the papers of the late Don Bradley and have since been donated to the South Western Circle by Mrs Ann Bradley (together with others of Don's records) which have been invaluable in preparing the text of this book.

For the provision of photographs, I am indebted to all those photographers whose material has found its way into my own collection over many years, in many cases with no record of the source. Richard Casserley has supplied prints from the H.C. Casserley collection, Nick Grant of the Ian Allan organisation allowed me free access to the company's archive and Mike King has supplied prints from the Ted West collection, which he holds on behalf of the South Western Circle. Rod Blencowe has supplied prints from his collection and has also printed some of my own negatives. John Harvey has produced scans from his collection to fill some of the gaps.

I am also most grateful to Eric Youldon and John Harvey who have long been researching the details of Southern locomotives. Both of these gentlemen looked through my draft texts and suggested many amendments, additions and corrections. John has delved into George Woodward's notebooks, recording details of every locomotive to leave Eastleigh works between 1928 and the 1960s, to clarify details of when some modifications were carried out. Roger Merry Price produced a set of Southern Railway headcode lists which has enabled me to identify many of the trains illustrated.

Peter H. Swift, Spondon, Derby March 2007.

Recommended reading:
S.C. Townroe, *King Arthurs & Lord Nelsons of the SR*, Ian Allan, 1949.
H. Holcroft, *Locomotive Adventure Volume 1*, Ian Allan, 1962.
H. Holcroft, *Locomotive Adventure Volume 2*, Ian Allan, 1965.
L. Tavender, *Livery Register No. 3 LSWR and Southern*, HMRS, 1970.
S.C. Townroe, *The Arthurs, Nelsons and Schools of the Southern*, Ian Allan, 1973
D.L. Bradley, *Locomotives of the Southern Railway, Part 1*, RCTS, 1975.
D.W. Winkworth, *Maunsell's Nelsons*, G. Allen & Unwin, 1980.
S.C. Townroe, *Arthurs, Nelsons & Schools at Work*, Ian Allan, 1982.
B. Haresnape, *Railway Liveries - Southern Railway*, Ian Allan, 1982.
J.E. Chacksfield, *Richard Maunsell An Engineering Biography*, Oakwood, 1998.
R. Derry, *The Book of the Lord Nelson 4-6-0s*, Irwell Press, 2005. Plus two photographic accompaniments.

Series Created & Edited by Jasper Spencer-Smith.
Design and artwork: Nigel Pell.
Produced by JSS Publishing Limited, P.O. Box 6031, Bournemouth, Dorset, England.
Colour Scanning: JPS Ltd, Branksome, Poole, Dorset, BH12 1DJ.

First published 2007

ISBN (10) 0 7110 3247 5
ISBN (13) 978 0 7110 3247 7

Published by Ian Allan Publishing

an imprint of Ian Allan Publishing Ltd, Hersham, Surrey KT12 4RG.
Printed in England by Ian Allan Printing Ltd, Hersham, Surrey KT12 4RG.

Code: 0706/B2

Visit the Ian Allan Publishing website at www.ianallanpublishing.com

Title spread: A 'Lord Nelson' heads past Eastleigh shed on a Union Castle Line boat train to Southampton in the mid-1950s. The 'Southampton Docks via Millbrook' headcode identifies it as running to the New (Western) Docks, until 1977. The Union Castle Line mailboats to South Africa left Berth 101 every Thursday at 4pm. (CR)

Photograph Credits
Colour-Rail (CR) and their photographers
D.H. Beecroft (DHB); T.J. Edgington (TJE); G.H. Hunt (GHH); J. Kinnison (JK); A. Morris (AM); National Railway Museum (NRM); Ray Oakley (RO); Pendragon Collection (PC); C.S. Perrier (CSP); Stephen Townroe (ST); P.B. Whitehouse (PBW).
Ian Allan Library (IA)
A. Ashley (AA); C.P. Boocock (CPB); C.E. Brown (CEB); A.C. Cawston (ACC); D. Cross (DC); J. Davenport (JD); J.C. Flemons (JCF); P. Hawkins (PH); C.C.B Herbert (CCBH); G.G. Jefferson (GGJ); B. Kimber (BK); J. Lucas (JL); F.E. Mackay (FEM); B. Morrison (BM); K.R. Pirt (KRP); G.H. Richardson (GHR); J.E. Tiely (JET) P. Ransome Wallis (PRW); G. Wheeler (GW).
Others
R.K. Blencowe (RKB) also RKB/A.C. Cawston (RKB/ACC) and RKB/W. Gilburt (RKB/WG); D.L. Bradley (DLB); H.C. Casserley (HCC); R.J. Harvey (RJH); Historical Model Railway Society (HMRS); Rail Archive Stephenson (RAS); Stephenson Locomotive Society (SLS); Peter H. Swift (PHS); A.E. West/South Western Circle (AEW/SWC); Author's Collection (AC).

INTRODUCTION

The Maunsell 'Lord Nelson' class locomotives were built
to work the small number of express trains on the
Southern Railway which were considered to be beyond
the capacity of the earlier 'King Arthur' class.

The sixteen 'Lord Nelson' class 4-6-0s were built at the Southern Railway's works, Eastleigh, Hampshire between 1926 and 1929. When new, the class failed to produce the supposed greater power than the existing 'King Arthur' class locomotives. Numerous modifications were tried to improve matters. Some were temporary and others permanent, some were restricted to a single locomotive and others applied to all, some were instigated by Richard Maunsell and others by his successor Bulleid. By the time these modifications had improved the performance of the 'Lord Nelsons' up to the initial expectations, World War Two had broken out. After the war, the class was overshadowed by the new Bulleid 'Pacific' locomotives. However, 'Lord Nelsons' were locomotives of great presence and one of their unusual design features caused them to produce a unique sound.

REQUIREMENTS

When the Southern Railway (SR) was formed in 1923, only one of its constituents, the London & South Western Railway (L&SWR), had any 4-6-0 express locomotives whilst the London Brighton & South Coast Railway (LB&SCR) worked much of the express traffic on short mainlines with large tank locomotives. The third constituent, the South Eastern & Chatham Railways (SE&CR), had been starved of investment by the cut-throat competition between its two constituents (the South Eastern Railway [SER] and the London Chatham & Dover Railway [LC&DR]) in the late 1800s. The SE&CR tracks were unable to carry more than 19-ton axle loading on the SER main line or $17^1/_2$ ton on the LC&D mainline. The company's board had appointed Maunsell to be their locomotive chief in 1913. He had formed a small team who were familiar with the best locomotive design practice of Swindon and Derby and had begun to modernise the SE&CR motive power, both by rebuilding and by new building, within the limited budget and axle loadings available. Boilers worked at higher pressures with Belpaire fireboxes and superheaters. Long-travel piston valves were fitted to rebuilt 4-4-0s, new 2-6-0s and one 2-6-4T.

Appointed Chief Mechanical Engineer (CME) of the newly formed Southern Railway, Maunsell was aware of the need for improved express locomotives. To fill the immediate need, his design team took Robert Urie's rugged 'N15' class 4-6-0 of the LS&WR and applied the design improvements which had proved successful on the his SE&CR locomotives. A total of 54 improved 'N15s', the 'King Arthur' class, were built between 1925 and 1927. By this time, the Dover mainline via Tonbridge was able to carry the class, and they

Above: No.852 *Sir Walter Raleigh* at Bournemouth West on a Waterloo train in 1936. Although not the best portrait of the locomotive, the photograph shows the Maunsell Dark Green livery and the red-backed name and number plates. (CR/JK)

Left: No.851 *Sir Francis Drake*, in Maunsell livery, heading a boat train via Maidstone at Ashford in 1938. (CR/CSP)

became the SR's standard express locomotive. Most of the Southern's express requirements were within the capacity of the class but there were a few services where it was apparent that something more powerful would be useful. An overall requirement of 500 tons (55,883Kg) at 55mph (88.5kph) start to stop was specified.

CONCEPTION OF THE LORD NELSON CLASS

The requirement to produce a more powerful locomotive within approximately the same overall weight as the 'King Arthur' class was a difficult, but not impossible, task. All Robert Urie's locomotives tended to be heavier than those of similar power built elsewhere. Maunsell's modifications to the Urie design had addressed the initial failure to produce potential power but had not attempted to reduce the locomotive's weight. The 'King Arthurs' were two-cylinder locomotives with cylinders as large as could be accommodated within the SR loading gauge. Only a small increase in power would have been possible with the boiler pressures in general use at the time.

In 1923, a committee of 10 senior railway Civil Engineers, including the SR's Chief Civil Engineer George Ellson, was set up to investigate the stresses imposed on bridges by different types of locomotives. Practical tests with a variety of locomotives showed clearly that the hammer blow effect from two-cylinder locomotives was worse than that imposed by multi-cylinder locomotives, Urie's L&SWR 4-6-0s being amongst the worst offenders. By 1920, most British locomotive designers were using either three or four cylinders

for large express locomotives. On a three or four-cylinder locomotive, the cylinders could be smaller, allowing a more powerful machine to be built within the loading gauge constraints. The reciprocating masses were lighter and would largely balance each other, although standard practice at the time was still to balance the reciprocating masses of each cylinder separately. The smaller balance weights required for the smaller pistons of a multi-cylinder locomotive caused less hammer blow on the track. The new 4-6-0 was therefore schemed as a four-cylinder machine with a Belpaire firebox, to the maximum dimensions which could be achieved within a $21^{1}/_{2}$ ton (25,909.3Kg) axle load, but this was reduced to $20^{1}/_{2}$ ton (20,829Kg) by Ellson during the design process.

Most four-cylinder locomotives were built with the pairs of inside and outside cylinders set at 180° to each other, so that reciprocating forces balanced each other but there were only four impulses per rotation of the wheels, as on a two-cylinder machine. In 1920, Harold Holcroft, one of Maunsell's headquarters team, presented a paper to the Institution of Locomotive Engineers in which he proposed setting the two pairs of cylinders at 135° to each other. The balancing is not as good, but still better than on a two-cylinder machine, but the machinery now produced eight impulses per rotation of the wheels, giving smoother power at the rail and a more even draught on the fire. This arrangement was first tried on a British locomotive by J.A. Hookham of the North Staffordshire Railway (NSR). In 1922, He built a single four-cylinder 0-6-0T for use on the steeply graded Potteries Loop line, serving the

various small towns which later formed the City of Stoke on Trent. When the NSR was absorbed by the LMS in 1923, the LMS was not interested in developing the idea; the locomotive was rebuilt with a tender in 1924 and scrapped in 1928.

Maunsell was clearly impressed by the theoretical advantages of the 135° crank setting and had one of Dugald Drummond's four-cylinder 4-6-0s from the L&SWR rebuilt to test the arrangement. This was 'P14' class No. E449, one of five locomotives built at Eastleigh in 1910. As built, the 'P14' had Stephenson's valve gear to the inside cylinders and Walschaerts gear outside. A combination of disparate valve gears, long and tortuous exhaust passages from the outside cylinders and an atrocious grate and ashpan design ensured that they were failures and, except for E449, were scrapped and replaced by new 'King Arthurs' in 1925. E449, the only one which had received a superheater, was renumbered E0449 and ran some trials on freight trains. It was then rebuilt with 135° crank

settings and further trials were carried out. These showed a 9.5% saving in coal consumption, apparently proving the advantage of the 135° crank setting, which was therefore adopted for the new 4-6-0s.

In 1925, Holcroft received a letter from Arturo Caprotti of the Italian State Railways (Ferrovie delle Stato [FS]) stating that he was fitting the 135° crank setting to a four-cylinder locomotive with Caprotti valve gear. This was probably one of four FS '685' class 2-6-2s rebuilt with Caprotti valve gear in 1924, although neither of two books on FS class locomotives consulted mentions any changed crank setting. Papers from the British Caprotti company now held by the Historical Model Railway Society (HMRS) state that the 135° crank setting was later adopted on five of 10 LMS (ex-L&NWR) Claughton class 4-6-0s rebuilt with Caprotti valve gear in 1928. The 135° crank setting was also applied to two of four 'XS' class 4-6-2s supplied by the Vulcan Foundry to the North Western Railway (India) in 1930. One of these had Caprotti, the other had Lentz-type valve gear.

Above: Guinea Pig. In 1924, Dugald Drummond's 'P14' class 4-6-0 E449 was rebuilt to try out Harold Holcroft's ideas for setting the cranks of a four-cylinder locomotive to give eight impulses each time the wheels went round. Whilst the rest of the class were scrapped and replaced by 'King Arthur' class locomotives, E0449 was modified with the cranks of the inside and outside cylinders set 135° apart and showed a 9.5% coal saving on freight duties. (AC)

Left: The prototype E850 running on trial in grey undercoat and unnamed at Eastleigh, August 1926. It is carrying the Waterloo to Bournemouth headcode which was discontinued in July 1928. E850 was the only 'Lord Nelson' to be built with L&SWR style lamp sockets. (RJH)

CHAPTER ONE

DESIGN, CONSTRUCTION & MAINTENANCE

The Southern Railway's prime express locomotive was
initially claimed to be the most powerful in Great Britain,
although the claim was never substantiated in practice
and they were soon eclipsed by locomotives which
were more powerful, both in theory and in practice.

As outlined in the previous chapter, the 'Lord Nelson' class was built to the maximum dimensions permitted by the SR's loading gauge and the axle load limitations. The boiler was the first to be built at Eastleigh with a Belpaire firebox, although Ashford had been building them for the previous 10 years. The firebox was longer than any used previously on the Southern. The rear part of the grate, above the rear coupled axle, was horizontal but the front part of the grate sloped down sharply, requiring a different firing technique from the Urie/Maunsell two-cylinder 4-6-0s, which had shorter grates with a continuous slope. On a large 4-6-0, with the boiler set as low as possible to fit within the British loading gauge, there was little alternative to the firebox arrangement provided on the 'Lord Nelsons'. The LMS and GWR used similar fireboxes on their large 4-6-0s, but in far greater numbers so their fireman quickly learned the firing technique. The firemen on the Southern's express passenger links spent most of their time on 'King Arthurs', 'Schools' class 4-4-0s or Bulleid 'Pacifics', all of which had straight sloping grates. Many of them never mastered the part flat, part sloping grate of the 'Lord Nelson' class.

The four cylinders were placed approximately in line above the bogie. The outside cylinders, slightly to the rear of the bogie centreline drove the second driving axle whilst the inside cylinders, slightly forward of the bogie centreline, drove the leading axle. The exhaust passages from the inside cylinders were direct but those from the outside cylinders had a double bend over the inside valve chest. The 135° crank setting necessitated four sets of Walschaerts valve gear. The bogie, with independent coil-spring suspension for each axle, was a new design. The bogies of the Urie/Maunsell two-cylinder 4-6-0s all had equalising beam suspension. The cab, with a single window and a cutout in each side, was similar to that used on Maunsell's L1 class 4-4-0, introduced three months earlier. The driver was on the lefthand side of the footplate.

CONSTRUCTION

Maunsell wisely decided to build a single prototype of the new 4-6-0, to enable any potential faults to be eliminated before constructing a fleet of untried locomotives. He had acted in a similar manner with his 2-6-0 and 2-6-4T designs for the SE&CR in 1917. The prototype four-cylinder 4-6-0 was ordered from Eastleigh works to order No. E124, on 29 May 1925. This order replaced the last of an existing order for 15 'King Arthur' class 4-6-0s.

Above: When the Brighton line was electrified in 1933, the ex-LB&SCR 'Remembrance' class 4-6-4Ts were rebuilt as 4-6-0s for the Bournemouth line. In the absence of a good colour photograph from the front of a 'Lord Nelson' in Maunsell livery, No. 2329 *Stephenson* has to act as a replacement, at Bournemouth Central on the up day mail train in 1936. Behind the tender are a Southern timber- bodied bogie luggage van and an ex-L&SWR Post Office van. (CR/JK)

Left: No. 864 *Sir Martin Frobisher* at Waterloo, July 1939. Livery is Bulleid light Malachite Green with black edging and yellow lining. (CR/CSP)

Right: The cab of a 'Lord Nelson' class 4-6-0. The Driver's position is on the left, shown by the handwheel of the reverser, with the vacuum brake control above. The regulator handle is double ended, so that the fireman can operate it in an emergency. As on most 20th century British locomotives, except on the GWR, the fireman must work left handed. The operating lever for the firedoor is placed so that a considerate driver can help his mate by opening and closing the door. (AC)

The new locomotive E850 was completed at Eastleigh Works on 11 August 1926. Initial trials and running in were carried out from Eastleigh shed, with the locomotive in grey undercoat and nameless. After painting, it was then sent to Nine Elms for trial running on the Western section mainlines to Bournemouth, Portsmouth and Exeter before being transferred to Battersea for trials on the Dover boat trains.

Although these trials indicated that the locomotive was not reaching expected performance in service, order No E157 was placed for 10 more locomotives on 13 March 1927, with only very minor differences from

the prototype. As with the initial order, this order also replaced an existing order for 10 more 'King Arthurs'. Locomotives E851 to E860 were completed at Eastleigh between June 1928 and April 1929. A final five locomotives were built to order No E348, placed on 23 March 1928. Locomotives E861 to E865 were completed between September and November 1929.

The Southern Railway's active publicity department ensured that the public was aware of the new locomotives. It was decided to name them after naval leaders of the past and, from the name applied to the prototype locomotive, they

Left: E850 *Lord Nelson* leaving Salisbury on a murky 2 April 1927 during test running on the 10.30 Exeter to Waterloo. An indicator shelter is fitted to protect the test crew. A speed recorder is fitted to the rear coupled wheels, with a drive similar to that used on the recorders fitted ten years later. (IA/ACC)

Left: E850 *Lord Nelson* at Dover circa 1928. It is largely as built but now has lamp irons inserted into L&SWR style sockets, to enable it to carry standard Eastern Section lamps and route code discs. It carries the Victoria to Dover via Tonbridge headcode, which placed the smokebox side disc right in the fireman's view of the line ahead. (HMRS)

were known as the 'Lord Nelson' class. Generally, the Southern's locomotive classifications followed the system used by the SE&CR, with a single letter for each basic type and a number suffix for variants and rebuilds. The 'Lord Nelsons' received the two letter classification LN; the only other Southern locomotives classified in this way were the later Bulleid 'Pacifics'. On the basis of its theoretical tractive effort of 33,300 lbf (Pounds force), the Southern publicity department claimed the new locomotive to be the most powerful express locomotive in Britain. However, the 'Lord Nelsons' as built were never a match for either the Great Western Railway (GWR) 'Castles', with a theoretical 31,625 lbf tractive effort or the LNER's 'A1' with 29,835 lbf. Within a year, the GWR had improved on this with the new 'King' class, fitting smaller driving wheels than the previous standard to push the tractive effort over the magic 40,000 lbf figure.

MAINTENANCE

Maintenance might seem irrelevant in a book dealing primarily with the external appearance of locomotives, but an understanding of maintenance procedures does explain why and

Above: Apple green liveried No. 30864 *Sir Martin Frobisher* in Southampton Docks after working a Royal Train in July 1948. The cylinders are now green. (CR)

Right: No. 855 *Howard of Effingham* at Woking, September 1939. Livery is light Malachite Green with black edging and yellow lining. The pre-war Bulleid-style tender gilt lettering is shown clearly. (CR/ST)

Above: Apple green liveried No. 30856 *Lord St. Vincent* leaving Poole on the Weymouth portion of a down train formed of the 'plum and spilt milk' set of carriages in August 1948. In the background, a 700 class 0-6-0 in clean Bulleid black livery waits to give assistance to up trains on Parkstone bank. (CR/PC)

Left: Apple Green liveried No. 30856 *Lord St. Vincent* leaving Eastleigh in October 1948. (CRST)

The driver of E850 *Lord Nelson* goes round with his oilcan at Eastleigh shed. The exhaust steam pipe from the vacuum ejector runs above the handrail and turns directly into the smokebox, to exhaust via the chimney. On the rest of the class, it had a downward joggle before entering the smokebox. That on E850 was modified, probably at the first General Overhaul. (IA/CEB)

when many changes to the appearance of the locomotives occurred. Class A overhauls, classified General Overhauls in British Railways days, occurred approximately every two years and took about a month. At a Class A overhaul, the locomotive would be lifted off its wheels, worn or damaged components brought back to standard and modifications would be carried out. The boiler was usually replaced by one which had previously been overhauled and the job would be finished by a full repaint into the current livery.

Class B (Intermediate) overhauls were carried out at approximately the halfway stage between Class A overhauls. Class C (Unclassified) repairs were carried out to rectify accident damage or other defects and might require a locomotive to go to the main works if the work was beyond the capability of the running sheds. Intermediate or unclassified repairs might be completed by touching up the paintwork or renumbering. Occasionally, locomotives were sent to main works specifically for painting, a Class D repair.

Overhauls and major repairs to the 'Lord Nelson' class locomotives were always carried out at Eastleigh works. Although their performance did not match expectations initially, there was never any doubt about their reliability in service. They were scheduled to run 90,000 miles (144,837km) between Class A (General) Overhauls, compared with 80,000 miles (128,744km) for the 'King Arthurs' and 70,000 miles (112,651km) for the 'Schools' class 4-4-0s. Despite the weight saving exercise at the design stage, they were almost immune from the problems of frame cracking which bedevilled so many British built plate framed steam locomotive types. The 90,000 miles (144,837km) between overhauls was frequently exceeded. In 1955, No. 30855 was shopped for a General Overhaul with a recorded mileage of 207,873 miles (334,530km) since the previous General Overhaul.

For the sixteen 'Lord Nelson' class locomotives, 19 boilers were built. Locomotives E850 to E860 were built with boilers numbered 850 to 860, boiler 860 being 10in (25.4cm) longer than the others. When locomotives E861 to 865 were built, Eastleigh had stopped giving boilers the number of the locomotives on which the boiler was first used. Six boilers 817 to 822 were built, the additional one being fitted to the prototype locomotive E850, allowing boiler 850 to be overhauled as the spare boiler. A further spare boiler 1234 was built in 1934. The nineteenth boiler was an experimental one with a round-topped firebox, numbered 1063 and fitted to No. 857 in 1937.

Above: E853 *Sir Richard Grenville* as built. The joggle in smokebox end of the vacuum ejector exhaust steam pipe is clearly visible. E853 carried an LB&SCR-style double lamp iron on the left side of the buffer beam, allowing the smokebox side disc to be clear of the fireman's view of the line. E852 and E853 ran initially with a 4000-gallon six-wheel tender. (AC)

Below: E857 *Lord Howe* at Battersea shed in the late 1920s, showing the 'standard' appearance of the first batch of 'Lord Nelsons', although only E851 and E854 to E857 were built with flat-sided bogie tenders. (IA)

Left: Apple Green liveried No. 30864 *Sir Martin Frobisher* arriving at Southampton Docks on a Royal Train, July 1948. For the short journeys on the Southern, it was usual to use Pullman cars for Royal trains, rather than the special Royal saloons. (CR/ST)

Left: No. 30850 *Lord Nelson* passing Eastleigh on a down boat train, 7 April 1960. A Pullman buffet car, displaced from the Hastings line and repainted green, has been added to eight-car train set 354. This comprises two BR standard brake 2nds, three Bulleid corridor 1st and three Bulleid open 2nds. (PHS)

Left: E853 *Sir Richard Grenville* nearing completion at Eastleigh works, 12 August 1928. The front drop of the running plate and the cover over the front of the inside valve chest have yet to be fitted. This allows the forward location of the inside cylinders to be seen. (HCC)

CHAPTER TWO

MODIFICATIONS

In an attempt to improve performance, Maunsell's design team applied a number of modifications to the 'Lord Nelson' class, some to a single locomotive and others to all of them. Further changes were made by Bulleid.

It was apparent as soon as the 'Lord Nelson' class locomotives were in service that they were not reaching their expected level of performance. In retrospect, it is clear that the main problems were with the draughting, exacerbated by the difficulty of firing the long, part flat part sloping, grate.

Maunsell Modifications

Steam locomotive design was never an exact science and in the 1920s, even the improved knowledge gained from more scientific testing methods from the 1930s to 1950s was not available. Maunsell's team started looking for solutions to the problems and a number of major modifications were carried out on single locomotives, all with negligible effect on their performance.

Smaller Driving Wheels on E859 Lord Hood

To provide improved performance on the gradients of the Eastern section main lines, E859 was built with 6ft 3in (1.90m) diameter driving wheels in place of the standard 6ft 7in (2.01m). Theoretically, this would produce a 5% increase in tractive effort but, in practice, this increase could be achieved by adjustment of the reverser

and regulator. No others were rebuilt but E859 retained small driving wheels until withdrawal. Structurally, the locomotive does not appear to have been altered, the correct ride height presumably being achieved by adjustment of the spring hangers with the cylinder centreline set 2in (51mm) above the wheel centres. The greater clearance between the driving wheels and the splashers is apparent in some photographs, as is the misalignment between the piston rod and the axle centrelines.

Longer Boiler on E860 Lord Hawke

The length of the boilers on the 'Lord Nelson' class had been reduced from that originally proposed, to achieve the weight limits imposed by the Civil Engineer. To improve the steaming capacity, E860 was built with a boiler of the length originally proposed, 10in (25.4cm) longer than standard. This had virtually no effect on the steaming capacity but increased the weight on the front of the locomotive and resulted in poor riding at speed. This boiler remained on No. 860, (apart from the period between October 1936 and August 1937) until 1955. It was then fitted to No. 30855, followed by No. 30852 in 1958. Whilst No. 860 was fitted with Maunsell-type cylinders, it was immediately recognisable by the

Above: No. 30852 *Sir Walter Raleigh* passing Winchfield on a Waterloo to Bournemouth express in August 1959. (CR)

Left: No. 30853 *Sir Richard Grenville* arriving at Basingstoke on a through train from the Reading line, 10 August 1960. (CR)

straight vertical front to the smokebox, which was in line with the casing over the valve chest of the inside cylinders. No photographs have been absolutely identified as showing No. 860 with a standard boiler in the period 1936/37. It may have carried a standard smokebox at this time but may have retained the forward set smokebox, extended rearwards to meet the boiler. After Bulleid-type cylinders and extended smokeboxes were fitted to the 'Lord Nelsons', all the modified locomotives had a straight smokebox front and this boiler could only be recognised by the joint between boiler and smokebox being further forward than on the standard boilers.

A study of the Engine Record Card (ERC) for No. 860 clearly shows the shortened overhaul duration allowed by having spare boilers. Whilst most A overhauls on 'Lord Nelsons' took approximately a month, No. 860 was in Eastleigh works for over five months for

Above: E859 *Lord Hood* as built. E858 to E860 were coupled initially to Urie-style tenders from 'S15' class 4-6-0s. E859 was built with smaller (6ft 3in[1.9m]) driving wheels. (AC)

Below: No. 30859 *Lord Hood* at Weymouth GWR shed on 23 June 1957. By placing a straight edge along the axle centres, the offset between the piston rod and axle centreline is clearly visible. (AEW/SWC)

an A overhaul in 1939 and four months in 1948. Other A overhauls on No. 860 only took approximately one month, presumably an inspection of the boiler *in situ* showed that no work was needed which required its removal from the locomotive.

SMOKE DEFLECTORS

The first 11 locomotives E850 to E860 were built without smoke deflectors. Smoke deflector plates had proved necessary on the 'King Arthur' class, to prevent the exhaust from dropping down over the boiler and obscuring the driver's view of the line. After a number of trials on 'King Arthurs', a satisfactory design had been produced and was fitted to all the 'Lord Nelson' in 1929 and 1930. The exact date is not known for some locomotives. The last five 'Lord Nelsons' E861 to E865 were built with smoke deflectors.

Left: E860 *Lord Hawke* at Bournemouth West on a Waterloo express at an unrecorded date, but after March 1934, when the headcode was changed. E860 now has smoke deflectors and repositioned lamp irons but retains the grab rail on the left side of the smokebox door. Behind the snifting valve, a double line of banding is faintly visible between the boiler and the smoke-box. This could indicate that No. 860 is running with a standard 'Lord Nelson' boiler 850, carried between December 1936 and July 1937. (AC)

180⁰ CRANK SETTING ON No. 865 *SIR JOHN HAWKINS*

All the 'Lord Nelsons' were built with 135° between the cranks of the leading and centre driving axles but Maunsell must have had doubts as to whether this was the best arrangement. In December 1933, locomotive No. 865 was altered to the conventional 180° setting and gained a reputation for being a 'strong' locomotive. As long as wheel-to-rail adhesion permitted it, four large tugs' per rotation of the wheels might get a train rolling quicker than 8 small tugs and would certainly have been more noticeable at slow speed than on the rest of the class. This advantage would only apply at low speeds and No. 865 was reported to use 2 to 4 lbs (.91 to 1.82Kg) more coal per train mile, or a 5% to 7% increase. Whilst this was less than the coal saving showed by E0449 on trials, it did tend to confirm the reduced coal consumption of the 135° crank setting. No. 865 retained the altered setting but no others were changed. It could be recognised by the square-ended balance weights on the driving wheels and, audibly, by a slower, heavier, exhaust beat.

ROUND TOP FIREBOX BOILER ON No. 857 *LORD HOWE*

Shortly before his retirement, Maunsell was planning new larger locomotives, including 4-6-2 passenger and 4-8-0 freight locomotives. To test the type of boiler which he had in mind for these locomotives, one was built and fitted to No. 857 *Lord Howe* in January 1937. It was built from nickel steel and had a round-topped firebox, extending into a long combustion chamber. It was no bigger than the boilers already fitted to the 'Lord Nelsons' but was pitched higher, making the locomotive

Below: E860 *Lord Hawke* at Nine Elms, 22 March 1930. The longer boiler on E860 is apparent. The whole smokebox, including the snifting valves, has moved forward 10in (25.4cm) but the relative positions of the live-steam pipe, chimney and vacuum ejector pipe to the cylinders have not changed. (HCC)

Above: Although numbered and named E850 *Lord Nelson*, this is E861 *Lord Anson*, at Eastleigh works before going to Liverpool as the Southern Railway's exhibit at the Liverpool & Manchester Railway 150th Anniversary celebrations. The polished tyres were repainted black before E861/E850 went to Liverpool. It is likely that any photograph of 'E850' with polished steel tyres and axle ends is actually E861. (AC)

Right: E865 *Sir John Hawkins* as built. The last five 'Lord Nelsons', E861 to E865, were built with smoke deflectors and with the smokebox side lamp irons raised up, putting a disc in these positions more in the crew's view of the line than before. The small grab rail on the frame, which would have been behind the lamp if fitted, has been replaced by hand-holds in the smoke deflectors and stanchions adjacent to the buffer beam lamp. (IA)

look bigger. The planned 4-6-2, for which a weight diagram was issued, would have had a wide firebox and a small-wheeled 4-8-0 locomotive could have had a deep, straight grate. To fit onto the 'Lord Nelson' chassis, the experimental boiler had to have the 'Lord Nelson's' part flat, part sloping grate. The steaming capacity of the boiler was worse than the originals and the riding of the locomotive was poor as the weight at the front of the locomotive was increased. As with No. 860, the smokebox was moved forward so that the front face was in line with the cover over the front of the inside valve chests. The experimental boiler was carried by No. 857 until September 1941 then from January 1943 to February 1945, in three separate phases, the second and third of which were in Bulleid's days but are listed here for completeness:

- January 1937 to June 1939; Maunsell-type cylinders, original chimney and Maunsell Dark Green livery.

- October 1939 to July 1941 Bulleid-type cylinders, Lemaître exhaust and Malachite Green livery
- January 1943 to Feb 1945, Bulleid-type cylinders, Lemaître exhaust and Black livery

Between September 1941 and November 1942 and from March 1945, No. 857 carried a standard 'Lord Nelson' boiler. During the first two phases with the round-topped boiler, No. 857 carried cranked smoke deflector plates but during the third phase, straight ones were carried, having been fitted with the standard boiler in September 1941.

CHIMNEYS

During the 1930s, a chimney without capuchon was fitted to 'Lord Nelson' class locomotives from time to time. The following are noted from dated photographs: No. 851 (April 1933, July 1937,

Left: No. 853 *Sir Richard Grenville* on the turntable at Dover between February 1930 and March 1932, when it ran with a Urie style tender. It has now been fitted with smoke deflectors and raised smokebox lamp irons and still carries its LB&SCR style double lamp iron on the fireman's side. (AC)

Left: No. E865 *Sir John Hawkins* approaching Martello Tunnel, Folkestone Warren, on an up boat train via Tonbridge in 1938. It now has the cranks set at the conventional 180^0 apart. The square ended balance weight on the leading coupled wheel is visible at the 4 o'clock position. The headcode for the route was changed in 1934. (RKB)

August 1938), No. 852 (June 1933), No. 853 (July 1935) and No. 858 (August 1937)

In order to improve the draughting of the 'Lord Nelsons', Maunsell obtained two different sets of Kylchap double blastpipe. The Kylchap was one of many devices produced over the years to increase the surface area of the exhaust steam which was drawing the combustion gases through the firebox and boiler. The original design by the Finnish engineer Kyösti Kylälä divided the single exhaust steam jet into four smaller jets. One was tested on a 'C' class 0-6-0 of the SE&CR in 1922. The French engineer André Chapelon added a petticoat above the Kylälä exhaust to produce the Kylchap. On the 'Lord Nelson' class, space constraints necessitated two separate Kylchap blastpipes exhausting into a double chimney. One set was fitted to No. 862 *Lord Collingwood* in August 1934. It did not materially improve steaming so the second set of Kylchap equipment was not used until after Bulleid had succeeded Maunsell as

CME. As part of his series of modifications to improve the 'Lord Nelsons', it was fitted to No. 865 *Sir John Hawkins* in June 1938. Visually, the presence of the double Kylchap blastpipe was shown by the double chimney. That on No. 862 had a capuchon whilst that on No. 865 had a raised lip all round. On No. 865, one Kylchap was fed from the outside cylinders, the other from the inside cylinders. Both Kylchaps were replaced by Lemaître exhausts in May and June 1939.

LAMP IRONS & FRONT HANDRAILS

E850 *Lord Nelson* was built with L&SWR-style lamp sockets; three across the buffer beam, one on either side of the smokebox and one towards the top of the smokebox door. Fairly early in service, lamp irons were placed in the sockets so that standard Eastern section lamps and discs could be carried. The sockets were replaced by standard lamp irons, probably at the same time as smoke

Above and right:
No. 857 *Lord Howe*, with the nickel steel boiler with a round topped firebox carried initially and from January 1937 to June 1939. No good drawing is known of the locomotive in this state. The line of 10 washout plugs show the length of the firebox and combustion chamber on this boiler. Note the joggled smoke deflector plates and the single snifting valve behind the chimney.
(AC [top] IA [right])

deflectors were fitted. L&SWR-style lamp sockets, with inserted lamp irons, were also carried on the rear of the five Urie-style bogie tenders which ran briefly with E852 and E853 also E858 to E860.

E851 to E860 were built with standard lamp irons, at the same positions as the sockets on E850. Early in service, E853 *Sir Richard Grenville* received an extended buffer beam lamp iron on the fireman's side. This lamp iron could carry both the lower and middle lamps or discs which had been standard practice on the London Brighton & South Coast Railway. It would have brought the offside middle disc down, out of the fireman's line of sight, whilst still being seen clearly to be in the middle position by signalmen. At that date, a disc in this position was used on the Victoria to Dover boat trains via

Right: No. 851 *Sir Francis Drake* approaching Bromley on an up boat train via Tonbridge, 14 April 1933. No. 851 now has smoke deflectors and repositioned smokebox lamp irons, placing the disc out of the fireman's view of the line. It is also fitted with one of the chimneys without a capuchon. (HCC)

Tonbridge, Kent which is probably why the extended lamp iron was fitted only on the fireman's side.

When smoke deflectors were fitted, the smokebox sidelamp irons were moved upwards and E860 to E865 were built with this arrangement. A disc on the middle lamp irons was now even more in the line of sight of the driver and fireman. The sidelamp irons were therefore moved onto the smokebox door. E853 appears to have lost the double lamp iron at the same time. On the left side of the smokebox door was a small grabrail, used to pull open the door. In some cases, the offside lamp iron was located next to this grab rail but the rail was later removed as the lamp iron was equally good for pulling the door open. The transverse handrail on the smokebox doors was shortened during the 1930s, but later than the fitting of smoke deflectors.

On E850 to E860, small grabrails were placed on the main frames of the locomotive, above the front platform. This was to assist when climbing onto the front of the locomotive by the footsteps. When smoke deflectors were fitted, these grabrails were replaced by small vertical stanchions next to the sidelamp irons on the buffer beam and by small handholds in the front

edge of the smoke deflectors. The nearside stanchions were removed from some of the 'Lord Nelsons' in British Railways (BR) days, probably because the handholds in the front edge of the deflector plates fulfilled the same function. All appear to have retained the offside stanchion.

BOGIE SPRINGS & FRAMES

The bogie of the 'Lord Nelson' was a new design with independent coil springs to each axlebox. The same design of bogie was later fitted to the 'Schools' class 4-4-0s. The 'Schools' were inclined to pitch on poor track and there were problems with the bogie frames fracturing. Both these problems were rectified by fitting stiffer coil springs to the bogies and new side frames, with a straight lower edge compared to the shallow 'V' form to the lower edge of the original bogies. Both problems were less severe on the 'Lord Nelson' class; the longer coupled wheelbase would inhibit pitching and the weight on the bogie was less. However, all the 'Lord Nelsons' except for E851 received the modified bogies in due course. Unfortunately, the bogie is hidden by dark shadows in many photographs, so it is not easy to identify which bogie frame is fitted.

Above: No. 857 *Lord Howe*, with nickel steel boiler with round topped firebox, on a Dover to Victoria via Tonbridge boat train. The fireman seems to be having combustion trouble. With the longer boiler, the smokebox front is in line with the casing over the front of the inside valve chest. (RKB)

Right: No. 30850 *Lord Nelson* at Weymouth shed with GWR 2-6-0 6344 and a BR standard 4-6-0 for company, 29 July 1961. No. 30850 is fitted with AWS with the battery box in the less common location, alongside the rear splasher. (CR)

Right: No. 30850 *Lord Nelson* at Eastleigh in April 1962. (CR)

VACUUM PUMP

The 'Lord Nelson'–class locomotives were built with a vacuum pump, driven from the crosshead of the lefthand inside cylinder, to maintain brake vacuum whilst running. These were removed in the early 1940s. As the pump was not visible from the side of the locomotive, this is a detail only of interest to modellers in larger scale .

BULLEID MODIFICATIONS

The SR's new CME applied further modifications to the 'Lord Nelson'–class locomotives, which did overcome the main problems. When Oliver Bulleid succeeded Maunsell in 1937, he began an

immediate investigation into his predecessor's express locomotives. To enable the 'Lord Nelsons' to reach full potential, he tried out a number of modifications which brought considerable improvement to performance, although the awkward grate remained unchanged. Before the work was finished, the World War Two had started and by the time peacetime rail services were resumed, Bulleid's own locomotives had taken over the most important services.

CHIMNEYS

As has been described in the chapter on Maunsell's modifications, one of Bulleid's first actions was to fit the unused second Kylchap double blastpipe to

No. 865 *Sir John Hawkins* in June 1938. At the same time, No. 863 *Lord Rodney* was fitted with a fabricated wide diameter stovepipe chimney, initially with a conventional blastpipe but with the cap removed to give a wide jet. This did not work so, in November 1938, a series of trials with various arrangements of multiple jet blastpipes were started on No. 863 and also on Nos. 855, 856, 861 and 864. The wide chimneys on these four locomotives had a narrow lip added. After a number of variants had been tried out, a final version with five nozzles set in a ring, was adopted. This arrangement, with a wider lip to the chimney, was then fitted to all the 'Lord Nelson' class between April and December 1939. It was referred to as a Lemaître exhaust, as it bore some

similarity to the arrangement developed by the Belgian engineer Maurice Lemaître of the Nord Belge Railway, although his arrangement also incorporated an adjustable central jet. Why the Lemaître worked whilst the Kylchap did not is unclear. Chapelon worked wonders with the Kylchap arrangement in France and the LNER also had considerble success with it, particularly on Gresley 'Pacifics' in British Railways service. The Kylchap arrangement required a lot of height, maybe the correct proportions could not be obtained inside the 'Lord Nelson' smokebox.

In 1956, No. 30852 *Sir Walter Raleigh* was fitted with a chimney from a Bulleid rebuilt 'Merchant Navy'-class locomotive, similar in shape to that fitted to the 'Lord Nelsons' but shallower. This

Right: No. 857 *Lord Howe* at Herne Bay, November 1939. It now has Bulleid-type cylinders, Lemaître exhaust and a self-trimming tender. Livery is light Malachite Green with black edging and yellow lining. The low light picks out the straight lower edge to the modified bogie frame. (IA/PRW)

chimney was a casting, whereas those on the 'Lord Nelson' classs were fabricated. It is not known whether this was a further attempt to improve performance or, more likely, because it was easily available whilst the 30 'Merchant Navy'-class locomotives were being rebuilt.

CYLINDERS

During his time as assistant to Sir Nigel Gresley on the LNER at Doncaster, Bulleid had been involved in the development of exhaust passages to give a freer exhaust. During tests with Gresley's 'P2' class 2-8-2, Bulleid had visited the French Railways test centre at Vitry, south of Paris, where André Chapelon was developing some of the most efficient, although complicated, steam loco-motives in the world. The exhaust passages of the 'Lord Nelsons' were such, that Chapelon would not have approved. Accordingly, new cylinders were designed and the first set were fitted to No. 851 *Sir Francis Drake*, which required new cylinders in April 1939. The first three sets of Bulleid-type cylinders had 8in (20.3cm) piston valves (as on

the Maunsell-type cylinders) but had smoother exhaust passages. Externally, the only change was that the live steam pipe to the outside cylinders was now covered by a squared casing which was entirely behind the smoke deflector plates, whilst the curved casing over the live-steam pipe, on Maunsell-type cylinders, projected through the deflector plates. The cylinders with 8in (20.3cm) piston valves were only fitted to No. 851, one of the two spare sets being fitted as a replacement in 1949.

After three sets of cylinders had been produced, the design was altered to include 10in (25.4cm) piston valves and a re-arranged steampipe and blastpipe arrangement. This necessitated the chimney being set forward and the smokebox front being extended level with the casing over the valve chest of the inside cylinders. The smokebox front was now straight to the front platform, as had previously been the case only on No. 860 and on No. 857 with the round topped boiler. The casing over the live steam pipe to the outside cylinders was completely behind the smoke deflectors, as on No. 851. After a number of the class had received the new cylinders, it was

The following table summarises the recognition points for the three type of cylinders:			
	Maunsell cylinders	**Bulleid cylinders with 8in (20.3cm) valves (851)**	**Bulleid cylinders with 10in (25.4cm) valves**
Line of smokebox and valve chest casing	Stepped (Straight on No. 860 and No. 857 with boiler 1063	Stepped	Straight
Live-steam pipe casing by Smoke Deflectors	Rounded, projects through plates	Squared behind plates	Squared behind plates

realised that they were not producing any marked improvement on the Maunsell-type and new cylinders were subsequently only fitted when required. Nos. 30853, 30858 and 30864 did not receive Bulleid-type cylinders until British Railways days and No. 30863 retained the Maunsell-type cylinders throughout.

INJECTOR

The 'Lord Nelsons' were built with a Davies & Metcalfe-type exhaust steam injector below the footplate. In March 1938, this was replaced on No. 858 *Lord Duncan* by a Monitor-type live-steam injector. This gave improved reliability but did not give the energy saving of the exhaust steam injector. No more were fitted in SR service but others were changed in British Railways days.

SNIFTING VALVES

The Maunsell-type superheaters, which were fitted to all the 'Lord Nelson'-class locomotives, had two snifting (anti-vacuum) valves, mounted either side of the smokebox behind the chimney. These were removed in the late 1940s. The experimental boiler fitted to No. 857 *Lord Howe* had a single snifting valve behind the chimney, which remained until the boiler was taken out of service.

SPEED RECORDER

Bulleid had experienced the use of speed recorders on locomotives on the LNER and decided to try out the equipment on the Southern. All the 'Lord Nelson' class and a number of other express locomotives were fitted with a French-manufactured Flamân speed recorder in 1938 and 1939. The speed recorder was located under the fireman's seat and recorded the speed of the locomotive on a paper roll. The drive to the speed recorder was taken from the crankpin of the rear right-hand driving wheel to a gearbox mounted on a bracket under the running plate. From this gearbox, a horizontal shaft drove the speed recorder. The equipment remained in use until 1940 to 1941.

Above: No. 30851 *Sir Francis Drake*, newly overhauled at Eastleigh in September 1958. Note the heraldically incorrect facing first (small) totem. The short smokebox, with a projecting casing over the inside valve chest, is apparent. (CR)

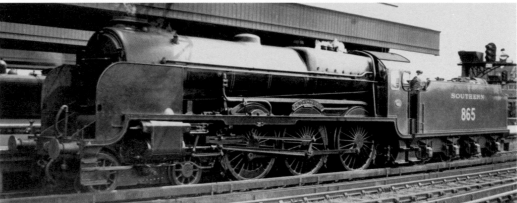

Right: No. 865 *Sir John Hawkins* at Waterloo. It was fitted with the second double Kylchap exhaust in June 1938. On No. 865, the front chimney took the exhaust from the inside cylinders and the rear chimney from the outside cylinders. (RJH)

Right: No. 856 *Lord St. Vincent* at Folkestone Junction in 1938. A large diameter stovepipe chimney with a narrow rim was fitted in November 1938, in connection with the multiple jet blastpipe trials. It is in Olive Green livery with green edging and yellow lining. (RKB)

Left: No. 30852 *Sir Walter Raleigh* at Eastleigh in October 1953, polished up to take guests to the wedding of Lord Montagu of Beaulieu. It is in BR Dark Green with 8in (20.3cm) cabside numerals, no power classification and first large totem on the tender. (CR/ST)

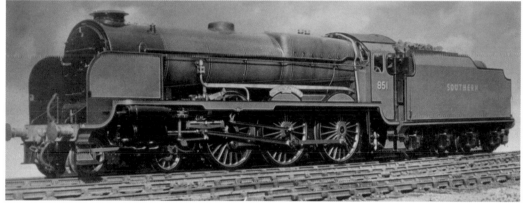

Left: No. 851 *Sir Francis Drake*. In June 1939 it received a Lemaître exhaust and the first set of Bulleid-type cylinders. These had 8in (20.3cm) piston valves and were retained (although with a replacement set from 1949) along with the short smokebox, until withdrawal. (IA)

Left: No. 865 *Sir John Hawkins* was fitted with the final form of Lemaître exhaust, with a wide-lipped chimney, in June 1939. At the same time, it was repainted in Malachite Green with black edging and yellow lining but retained its low sided tender until September 1940. (SLS)

Right: No. 863 *Lord Rodney* at Eastleigh in late 1938. No. 863 had been fitted with a large diameter chimney, with a single large diameter blast-pipe, in June 1938. At that time, it was still in Maunsell livery but, as seen here, was repainted in Bulleid's first experimental Olive Green livery in November 1938. This was at the same time as trials with multiple jet blastpipes were started. The stovepipe chimney has only a beading around the top. The drive to the Flamen speed recorder can be seen in front of the rear drop of the running plate. (AC)

In the late 1950s, British Railways began to install speedometers on express locomotives and 10 'Lord Nelsons' were fitted between 1959 and 1960. The equipment were driven from the crankpin of the left-hand rear coupled wheel by means of a gearbox and a flexible cable. They indicated the speed on a dial in the cab.

▍ AUTOMATIC WARNING SYSTEM ▍

In the late 1950s, BR's Automatic Warning System (AWS) was being installed on the mainlines,

including parts of the Southern region. A receiver on the locomotive picked up signals from electro-magnets in the track at each signal. At a clear signal, a bell rang in the cab. If the signal was at caution, the vacuum brake was applied, the inrush of air sounding a horn in the cab. All the 'Lord Nelson'-class locomotives except No. 30865 were fitted with AWS between 1959 and 1962. The receiver was mounted on the bogie, with a protective 'bash' plate below the buffer beam to prevent damage from the coupling. A battery box was placed on the left-hand running plate. On the first locomotives

Right: No. 30856 *Lord St Vincent* in the works yard at Eastleigh, 18 September 1960, following an overhaul during which the British Railways AWS was fitted. The low angle allows the AWS receiver to be visible, silhouetted between the leading bogie wheels. The 'bash plate' behind the coupling prevents damage from a swinging coupling. (PHS)

fitted, this was located towards the outer edge of the running plate, between the centre and rear splashers. On locomotives fitted with AWS after August 1960, the box was mounted alongside the rear splasher. It is thought that the latter location was used on Nos. 30850, 30851, 30852, 30856, 30860 and 30862.

WATER TREATMENT

In April 1959, a start was made in providing 'Lord Nelson'-class locomotives with the BR-type water treatment system, in which blocks of chemicals were placed in a feeder container on top of the tender. Apart from the container the only visual indication on the locomotive was the addition of a yellow disc painted on the cabside, below the number. On the Western Region, this indicated a locomotive with less than 16 ton (16,257Kg) axle load, so the yellow disc was replaced by a yellow triangle in 1961. In some late photographs of 'Lord Nelsons'-class locomotives, no water treatment symbol is carried.

CHAPTER THREE

TENDERS

For most of the time in service, all 'Lord Nelsons'
ran with similar tenders but some locomotives
ran with two other types in early years.

For most of their service life, the class ran with flat-sided 5000-gallon (22,730 litre) bogie tenders, rebuilt between 1937 and 1940 with raised sides and self trimming bunkers. Initially, some locomotives ran with a 4000-gallon (18,184 litre) six wheel tenders or with a Urie-style 5000-gallon (22,730 litre) bogie tender with turned out copings.

FLAT-SIDED BOGIE TENDER

When E850 *Lord Nelson* left Eastleigh works in August 1926, it was coupled to the first of a new type of 5000-gallon (22,730 litre) bogie tender. This was developed from the bogie tender introduced by Robert Urie on his L&SWR 4-6-0s but had flat sides, in the style of the 3500-gallon (15,911 litre) six-wheel tender which Maunsell had used at Ashford on his 'N' class 2-6-0s. The bogies were to the Urie pattern but with arched cut outs in the lower edge of the sideframes. On top of the tender, behind the coal space, were three vacuum reservoirs. With the vacuum brake, or with a single pipe air brake, difficulties could be had in releasing the brake immediately after it had been applied. The vacuum stored in these assisted a quicker brake release. The footsteps at each corner of the tender had curved backing plates, to match those of the locomotive.

The tender of E850 was numbered 1000 in August 1927.

URIE-STYLE BOGIE TENDER

In 1927, following construction of E850, Eastleigh works built two batches of Maunsell's improved version of Urie's 'S15' class goods 4-6-0. Locomotives E828 to E832, from the first batch of these, were built with Urie-style bogie tenders with turned out copings and coal retaining plates, but with the modified bogies and additional vacuum reservoirs as fitted to the flat-sided tender built with E850. These were the last locomotives to be built at Eastleigh with L&SWR style lamp sockets. The second batch of 'S15s', E833 to E837, were built with flat-sided bogie tenders, like that coupled to E850 but with conventional lamp irons. All 10 of these tenders would soon enter the 'Lord Nelson' story.

SIX-WHEELED TENDER

When the second batch of 'Lord Nelsons', E851 to E860, were built, ten 4000-gallon (18,184 litre) six-wheeled tenders were built with them. The main use of the class was on the Dover boat trains, for which 4000 gallons (18,184 litre) of water would be sufficient. This was another new design of tender,

Left: Rear of the tender of preserved No. 850 *Lord Nelson* at Liverpool Road Station, Manchester, 9 August 1980. (PHS)

Above: The prototype flat-sided bogie tender 1000, for No. 850 *Lord Nelson*, in Eastleigh Works, 1926. Note the arrangement of the sandboxes on either side of the shovelling plate, the handbrake and the longitudinally set toolboxes. (RJH)

Right: Rear view of tender 1011 of E861 *Lord Anson*, but masquerading as E850 *Lord Nelson*, at Eastleigh Works before going to Liverpool for the Liverpool & Manchester 100th Anniversary exhibition. The curved edged footstep backing plates are angled out to merge with the running plate valance. The double water tank fillers and auxiliary vacuum reservoirs are clearly seen. (AC)

effectively a shortened version of the flat sided bogie tender built with E850. Although looking superficially similar to the Ashford-pattern 3500-gallon (15,911 litre) tender, they were built to Eastleigh dimensions with the tank wider, and set lower, than the Ashford design and did not have the cutouts in the frames of the Ashford design. This batch of tenders had straight edged footstep backing plates, as used on the earlier Urie tenders. Later tenders to this design had curved footstep backing plates.

EARLY TENDER EXCHANGES

Before any of the E851 to E860 series locomotives went to traffic, it was realised that coupling them to the 4000-gallon (18,184 litre) tender would preclude their use on the longer runs of the Western section. Accordingly, only E852 and E853 went to traffic with the six-wheel tender. The others were coupled to tenders from eight of the recently built 'S15' class. E851 and E854 to E857 received flat-sided tenders from 'S15' locomotives E833 to E837.

The chronology of tender exchanges and rebuilding is summarised as follows:				
Locomotive	Six-wheel tender	Urie-type tender	Flat-sided bogie tender	Self-trimming bunker
E850	none	none	August 1926	June 1939
E851	none	none	May 1928	June 1939
E852	July 1928	December 1929	June 1931	November 1937
E853	September 1928	February 1930	April 1932	September 1940
E854	none	none	October 1928	February 1939
E855	none	none	October 1928	August 1938
E856	none	none	November 1928	July 1940
E857	none	none	December 1928	October 1939
E858	none	February 1929	February 1932	May 1940
E859	none	March 1929	July 1932	January 1940
E860	none	April 1929	June 1931	December 1939
E861	none	none	September 1929	November 1938
E862	none	none	October 1929	April 1940
E863	none	none	October 1929	December 1940
E864	none	none	November 1929	January 1939
E865	none	none	November 1929	September 1940

E858 to E860 received Urie-style tenders from 'S15s' E828 to E830. Between 1929 and 1930, the six-wheeled tenders coupled to E852 and E853 were replaced by the Urie-style bogie tenders from 'S15' locomotives E831 and E832. Finally, between 1931 and 1932, the Urie-style tenders behind E852 and E853 also E858 to E860 were exchanged with flat-sided bogie tenders which had been running behind 'King Arthurs' E768 to E772. The third batch of 'Lord Nelsons' E861 to E865 always ran with flat-sided bogie tenders. Until the 1930s, Southern tender

numbers were likely to be changed when moved from one locomotive to another. In the early 1930s, the flat-sided bogie tenders attached to locomotives E851 to E865 were numbered 1001 to 1015, in order, following tender 1000 of E850.

SELF-TRIMMING BUNKER

The 'Lord Nelsons' were difficult locomotives to fire and the task of the fireman was not eased by the need to move coal forward from the rear of the long tender. Accordingly, shortly before

Left: A 4000-gallon six wheeled tender of E853 *Sir Richard Grenville* at Longhedge, 1 June 1929. The similarity to the flat-sided bogie tender is clear but there is only a single tank filler. The footstep backing plates are straight edged and do not merge into the platform valance. The tender carries an E853 plate but no buffer beam numerals. (HCC)

Right: No. 30854 *Howard of Effingham* at Eastleigh, October 1951, newly repainted in British Railways Dark Green livery. Note the red backed nameplates, 10in (25.4cm) cabside numerals with the A power classification below and the first large totem. (CR)

Right: On 20 July 1952, No. 30854 *Howard of Effingham* was heading an up semi-fast train, routed over the up local line from Eastleigh to allow a late running boat train to overtake. The driver misread the signals and ran off the end of the line, where the two up tracks are reduced to one on the approach to Shawford station. I was taken to see No. 30854, still lying on its left side at the foot of the embankment, during the following week. Eastleigh shedmaster Stephen Townroe photographed the locomotive after it had been lifted upright, before being hauled back onto the embankment on temporary tracks. (CR)

Left: No. 30854 *Howard of Effingham* at Eastleigh, April 1960. AWS was fitted in October 1959. (CR)

Left: No. 30854 *Howard of Effingham* at Eastleigh, October 1958, in BR Dark Green livery with black backed nameplates, 8in (20.3cm) cabside numerals and the second tender totem. (CR)

Left: No. 30850 *Lord Nelson* near Woking on a short parcels train, 14 August 1962. (CR)

he retired, Maunsell had drawings prepared for a modification to the tender to make the coal bunker self trimming. The coal space was shortened and raised, with the floor of the bunker angled so that the coal at the rear fell forward as that in front was shovelled out. The sides were extended and turned in, to clear the loading gauge. A sleeve for fire-irons was placed along the driver's side of the bunker. At the same time, the Eastleigh-style toolboxes, with hinged lids, fitted at

the front of the tender were replaced by Ashford-style transverse lockers with hinged doors.

LATER TENDER EXCHANGES

Over the years there were a number tender exchanges between 'Lord Nelson'-class locomotives. For example, H.C. Casserley photographed No. 853 running with No. 863's tender in July 1935. This appears to have been a

Right: The practice of painting the locomotive number in large numerals on the tender was excellent, as long as tenders remained with their locomotives. No. 853 *Sir Richard Grenville* is running with the tender from No. 863, approaching Bromley on a Ramsgate to Victoria express on 14 July 1935. (HCC)

Left: No. 852 *Sir Walter Raleigh* was the first 'Lord Nelson' to have a self-trimming bunker added to the tender in November 1937. No. 852 is at Bournemouth Central on a Waterloo train in 1939. (RJH)

Left: No. 855 *Robert Blake*, with self-trimming tender, at Folkestone Junction, 25 June 1939. The coaling plants generally managed to deposit a considerable quantity of coal behind the self-trimming bunker, somewhat negating the object of the design. (HCC)

Below: Flat-sided bogie tender 1013 on E863 *Lord Rodney* passing Bromley on a down boat train, 7 August 1937. (HCC)

short term exchange and is not shown on the record cards. From the 1940s, tender exchanges, both at sheds and at works, became common on the 'Lord Nelsons' and the record cards show that only Nos. 851, 855, 859 and 863 ran from 1935 to withdrawal with the same tender throughout. This is in marked contrast to the 'King Arthurs', where tender changes were far less common apart from the brief use of flat-sided tenders in the late 1930s and 1940s, until the replacement of Drummond and six-wheel tenders by Urie tenders in the final years. As all the 'Lord Nelson' tenders were the same, these exchanges are only described where this resulted in livery changes. (See page 61.)

As the first 'Lord Nelsons' were withdrawn, two of the tenders were transferred to 'Schools' class locomotives, to improve their braking capability when on freight trains. Tender 1007 from No. 30854 went to No. 30921 in November 1961 and tender 1012 from No. 30865 went to No. 30912 in July 1961.

CHAPTER FOUR

LIVERIES

The 'Lord Nelson'-class was always finished in green except for a wartime period when they were painted black. The shade of the green and the style of lettering varied.

When new, the 'Lord Nelsons' were painted in Maunsell's Dark Green livery, with the locomotive's number on the tender. Bulleid introduced a variety of brighter liveries, some being carried by a single locomotive, before standardising on Malachite Green. After 1942, the class was painted black but the Malachite Green returned in 1946. In early BR days, there was considerable variety in lettering, and an experimental Apple Green livery, before British Railways Dark Green was adopted in 1949.

MAUNSELL SR LIVERIES

Boiler, cab, splashers, footplate valance, cylinders and tender sides were Dark Green with black edging, with a fine white line between the green and the black. The coal retaining plates on the Urie tenders were green, without the edging or lining. Boiler bands were black with a fine white line either side, but with only one white line at the rear of the smokebox. Similar banding was applied to the front and rear vertical edges of the green-painted cylinders, but this was replaced by a rectangular panel in late 1937 and was applied to Nos. 855, 862, 863, 865 and, probably, No. 858. Wheels were green, with black rims and axle ends.

The Southern Railway did not initially renumber inherited locomotives, but added a prefix to the number, A (Ashford) for ex-SE&CR locomotives, B (Brighton) for ex-LB&SCR locomotives and E (Eastleigh) for ex-L&SWR locomotives. New locomotives were numbered into the appropriate series for maintenance works, the 'Lord Nelsons' all having E prefix numbers. In 1931, the Southern abandoned prefixes. E series locomotives retained the existing number whilst 1000 was added to most A series numbers, 2000 to B series numbers and 3000 to L&SWR duplicate numbers. Isle of Wight locomotives retained the number series, with a W prefix.

The 'Lord Nelsons' were all delivered with L&SWR-style 6in (15.24cm) sans serif shaded gilt buffer beam numerals, with **NO.** to the left of the coupling and the number to the right. From around 1930, the gilt buffer beam lettering was replaced by 6in (15.24cm) yellow serif numerals with the E prefix to the left of the coupling and the number to the right. When the prefixes were abandoned, the **NO.** reappeared on the buffer beams, to the left of the coupling.

The locomotive's number was displayed on the cabside by an oval brass numberplate, $13^5/\!{}_8$in x $7^5/\!{}_8$in (34.6cm x 19.4cm) with the lettering SOUTHERN RAILWAY in an arc around the top of the plate with the number below and the prefix between. A third plate was attached to the rear of the tender body.

Above: No. 30854 *Howard of Effingham* approaching Eastleigh on an up boat train, 4 July 1961. As well as two maroon liveried luggage vans, one ex-LNER the other a BR standard GUV, two Pullman cars have been added to the green boat train set, the obvious one in position 4 and a green painted Hastings buffet car in position 8. (PHS)

Left: No. 30855 *Robert Blake* at Eastleigh, July 1957. It is in British Railways Dark Green with 8in (20.3cm) cabside numerals, black-backed nameplates and the first totem. (CR/TJE)

Top: E850 *Lord Nelson* in the Maunsell Dark Green livery at Battersea when new. The non-standard arrangement of the brake ejector pipe is clearly seen, as is the difference in the background colour of the nameplate (red) and the cabside numberplate (black). These details applied only on E850 when new. (AC)

Above: No. 855 *Robert Blake*, the second 'Lord Nelson' to receive a self-trimming tender in August 1938. (AC)

48

When the prefixes were abandoned, the E prefix on the cabside plates was removed and the numberplates on the rear of the tenders were replaced by transfer numerals. The backing colour of the nameplates and numberplates was red, using the same vermilion colour (with a tint of orange) as was used for the buffer beams, although it is thought that, when new, E850 *Lord Nelson* had green or black-backed numberplates.

Tender lettering comprised the word SOUTHERN, 9ft 9in (2.97m) long in elongated 6^{1}/$_{2}$in (16.5cm) serif letters.

The locomotive number was applied below it in 18in (46cm) block figures, with the 3in (7.6cm) E prefix in between. The lettering and numbers were in a Primrose colour. When the E-prefix was abandoned, the space between the number and the SOUTHERN lettering was reduced.

BULLEID LIVERIES

Between 1938 and 1942, Bulleid tried out an assortment of brighter liveries. In late 1938, four Eastern section 'Lord Nelsons' were repainted in a light Olive Green livery known as 'Dover Green' and a number of Bournemouth 'Schools' class were repainted in a bright green known as 'Bournemouth Green', later referred to as Malachite Green. Some carriages were also repainted in these colours, so that complete trains could be made up in the new liveries. After these trials, a variety of new liveries were applied to 'Lord Nelsons', 'Schools' and 'King Arthurs', before a slightly darker version of Malachite Green was adopted as standard in July 1940.

Livery variants were:

(a) Olive Green with dark green edging and yellow lining, Nos. 855, 856, 861 and 863 in November 1938.

Above: No. 863
Lord Rodney was one
of four of the class to
be repainted in
November 1938 in
Oliver Bulleid's first
experimental livery of
Olive Green with dark
green edging and
yellow lining . Wheels
and footstep backing
plates are green but
cylinders and smoke
deflectors are black. It
is fitted with an
experimental multiple
jet blastpipe. (IA)

Left: After the first
four 'Lord Nelsons' in
Olive Green, three
were repainted in
three further
experimental liveries
in early 1939. No. 864
Sir Martin Frobisher
was painted in
Maunsell Green with
Bulleid-style lettering
in January 1939.
At the same time,
it received an
experimental
multiple-jet blastpipe
and a self-trimming
bunker to the tender.
No. 864 on display
in the Bisley branch
bay platform at
Brookwood. (IA/JET)

(b) Maunsell Green with black edging and white lining, No. 864 in January 1939.

(c) Olive Green with black edging and white lining, No. 854 in February 1939.

(d) Light Malachite Green with black edging and white lining, No. 853 in April 1939.

(e) Olive Green with dark green edging and yellow lining, Nos. 852, 858 and 859 in April to May 1939.

(f) Light Malachite Green with dark green edging and yellow lining, Nos. 851, 862 and 863 in May to June 1939.

(g) Light Malachite Green with black edging and yellow lining, all except Nos. 851, 852, 853, 863 and 864 between June 1939 and May 1940.

(h) Olive Green with black edging and yellow lining, No. 852 in February 1940.

(i) Darker Malachite Green with black edging and yellow lining, all except Nos. 852, 859, 861 and 862 between July 1940 and March 1942.

Livery (b) was effectively the Maunsell livery, including green cylinders, with Bulleid-style lettering. On all the other liveries, the cylinders were unlined black. Smoke deflectors were black in liveries (a) to (d) and were lined green in liveries (e) to (h). In livery (e), the lower edge of the green panel came down to the running plate, with no bottom lining, on Nos. 852 and 859. On No. 858 in livery (e) and in liveries (f) and (i), the lower edge of the green panel was straight, above the line of the raised running plate. In all these liveries, the wheels and footstep backing plates were green.

In all the Bulleid liveries, the running number was applied to the cabside in place of the numberplate and the word 'SOUTHERN' was placed centrally on the tender side. The 9in (23cm)

Right: No. 30855
Robert Blake
between No. 30858
Lord Duncan and
Adams 4-4-2T
No. 30582, out of
use at Eastleigh.
No. 30855 was with-
drawn from service in
September 1959 and
scrapped at Eastleigh
in February 1962.
(CR)

Right: No. 30856
Lord St. Vincent, in BR
Dark Green with red
backed nameplates,
10in (25.4cm) cabside
numerals and the first
large totem on the
tender, on
an up train at
Bournemouth West
in August 1952.(CR)

Right: No. 30855
Robert Blake
approaching the
divergence of the
Bournemouth and
west of England lines
at Battledown on a
down Bournemouth
express in 1956.
An early Maunsell
corridor 3rd has been
added in front of a
Bulleid six-car dining
set in carmine and
cream, with green
carriages at
the rear. (CR)

Left: No. 30856 *Lord St. Vincent* on completion of a last General Overhaul at Eastleigh, 15 September 1960. No. 30856 is in BR Dark Green with 8in (20.3cm) cabside numerals and left-facing second totem on both sides of the tender. (CR)

Left: No. 30856 *Lord St. Vincent* is being coaled by a crane at Eastleigh in 1962, whilst the coaling plant was out of action. AWS was fitted in September 1960, with the battery box alongside the rear splasher. (CR)

Above: In February 1939, No. 854 *Howard of Effingham* was repainted in Olive Green with black edging and white lining and retained the single blastpipe but received a self-trimming bunker. No. 854 is passing Bromley on a down boat train via Tonbridge, 18 March 1939. (HCC)

Right: In April 1939, No. 853 *Sir Richard Grenville* was repainted in light Malachite Green with black edging and white lining. No. 853 was fitted with the standard type Lemaître exhaust at the same time, but retained the low-sided tender. (SLS)

sans serif block letters were initially gilt, with a fine body colour line inside the letters. Also 9in (23cm) shaded gilt numerals were applied to the locomotive bufferbeams, but some re-liveried 'Lord Nelson' class locomotives retained yellow serif bufferbeam numerals.

In September 1941, 'Sunshine'-style characters were introduced for both the numerals and the word 'SOUTHERN' on black locomotives. The characters were golden yellow with green shading and lining, with yellow highlights within the shading. When the green livery was re-introduced in 1946, similar characters but with black shading and lining were used. It is not thought that 'Sunshine'-style lettering was used on green repaints in the period 1941 to 1942.

Between May 1942 and April 1946, all the 'Lord Nelsons' were repainted in unlined black with green-shaded 'Sunshine'-style lettering.

From March 1946, Malachite Green began to be used again, to livery variant (i), with black-shaded 'Sunshine'-style lettering. Wheels were still generally green, but footstep backing plates were now black and the size of the bufferbeam numerals was reduced to 6in (15cm). All the 'Lord Nelsons' except for No. 862 were repainted green before nationalisation in 1948.

BRITISH RAILWAYS LIVERIES

With three exceptions, referred to below, for the first 18 months of British Railways ownership, the livery applied to the 'Lord Nelson' class was SR Malachite Green, but with various schemes of lettering. Generally, full repaints only occurred at full overhauls but partial repaints, such as adding 30xxx numbers, also occurred at light repairs. Generally, smoke deflectors and

Left: The next livery variant, in April to May 1939, reverted to the first experimental Olive Green with dark green edging and yellow lining, but with the addition of green smoke deflectors. On No. 852 *Sir Walter Raleigh*, shown, and No. 859 *Lord Hood*, the green on the smoke deflectors came down to the platform, with no bottom lining. Both locomotives received Lemaître exhausts at the same time. No. 852 already had a self-trimming bunker (AC)

Left: No. 858 *Lord Duncan* was also repainted in May 1939 in Olive Green with dark green edging and yellow lining but the green on the smoke deflectors was limited to a panel above the raised platform, setting the pattern for all further green repaints until the 1950s. Unusually, No. 858 has yellow serif buffer beam numerals but applied in Bulleid-type, without the **Nº**. The locomotive is at Waterloo during 1939, next to a carriage in Bulleid's Malachite Green livery. (IA)

wheels were green but, in June 1949, No. 30854 was repainted with black wheels and No. 30859 with black wheels and smoke deflectors. After the Dark Green had been introduced, Malachite Green No. 30850 was part repainted with black smoke deflectors in October 1949 and No. 30854 in April 1950.

Dates of renumbering were recorded on the Engine Record Cards. Amongst the partial repaints, s854, received an s-prefix to the number and Nos. 30858 and 30859, received British Railways numbers whilst still carrying 'SOUTHERN' on the tender. Early in 1948, British Railways tried out a number of experimental liveries on locomotives from all of the grouping companies. On the Southern, this included three of the class Nos. 30856, 30861 and 30864 in Apple Green with red, yellow and grey lining, similar to that used on the British

Railways lined-black livery but with yellow in place of cream.

Livery and lettering variants in use at the time the 'Lord Nelsons' received British Railways numbers were:

(j) Malachite Green with 'SOUTHERN' in 'Sunshine'-style Lettering No. 30858 in June 1948 and No. 30859 in February 1949.

(k) Malachite Green with 'BRITISH RAILWAYS' in 'Sunshine'-style lettering, s854 and 30856 in March to April 1948.

(l) Apple Green with 'BRITISH RAILWAYS' in Bulleid-style lettering with no shading, Nos. 30856, 30861 and 30864 in May – June 1948

(m) Malachite Green with 'BRITISH RAILWAYS' in Gill sans lettering, Nos. 30850, 30853, 30860, 30862 and 30865 in August to November 1948.

Above: No. 30857 *Lord Howe* on the 'Cunarder' boat train at the Ocean Terminal in Southampton Docks in 1956. BR Dark Green livery with 8in (20.3cm) cabside numerals and right facing second totem on the right side of the tender. (CR)

Right: No. 30857 *Lord Howe* at Eastleigh in 1959, in BR Dark Green with the second tender totem. (CR/NRM)

Right: No. 30857 *Lord Howe* on the Cunarder boat train at the Ocean Terminal in Southampton Docks in 1956. An LMS bogie luggage van in unlined carmine and a GWR one in brown are followed by an L&SWR 'Ironclad' brake first and another Southern carriage in green, one in carmine and cream, followed by Pullman cars. (CR/PW)

Left: No. 30857 *Lord Howe* at Eastleigh in 1959, in BR Dark Green with the second tender totem. (CR/NRM)

Left: No. 30857 *Lord Howe*, standing at Eastleigh shed in August 1960, having just come from the last General Overhaul at Eastleigh Works. No. 30857 now has left-facing second totem on both sides of the tender. (CR)

Right: Between May and June 1939, Nos. 851, 862 and 863 were painted in light Malachite Green with dark green edging and yellow lining. No. 851 *Sir Francis Drake* received a Lemaître exhaust, a speed recorder and a self-trimming bunker at the same time. (RAS)

Right: Apart from No. 852, which received Olive Green in February 1940, the Bulleid livery was standardised as Malachite Green with black edging and yellow lining in June 1939. Until May 1940, the light Malachite Green was used, but a slightly darker shade was used between July 1940 and March 1942. No. 864 *Sir Martin Frobisher* received the light version of this livery, and a Lemaître exhaust, in June 1939. No. 852 is waiting to leave Bournemouth West on a rather short all-Pullman Bournemouth Belle train to Waterloo. (AC)

(n) Malachite Green with no tender lettering, Nos. 30851, 30852, 30854 and 30855 between January and June 1949.

(o) British Railways Dark Green with large first totem, Nos. 30857 and 30863 between August and December 1949.

Note that Nos. 30854 and 30856 appear twice in the above list.

The BRITISH RAILWAYS in 'Sunshine'-style was produced by applying transfer letters where these were available from the existing SOUTHERN transfers, with the others letters handpainted. On the Apple Green locomotives, plain handpainted characters of Bulleid type were used. The cabside numerals were in 9in (23cm) Bulleid numerals (6in [15cm] on No. 30856 in Malachite Green) when 'Sunshine' or Bulleid-style lettering was used on the tender, and in 10in (25.4cm) Gill sans numerals when the tender was lettered in Gill sans or unlettered. Smokebox number plates were fitted from June 1948, but were also added during intermediate works visits, to locomotives in the earlier liveries. Probably starting with the repaints with unlettered tenders, the A power classification was moved from the front of the running plate valance to the cabside, below the number.

Left: No. 865 *Sir John Hawkins* was repainted in Malachite Green with black edging and yellow lining in June 1939, at the same time as receiving a Lemaître exhaust. No. 865 retained the low-sided tender until September 1940. The pre-war Bulleid lettering has a black line inside the gilt character but no shading. (IA)

Left: No. 852 *Sir Walter Raleigh* was the locomotive which received the last Olive Green repaint in February 1940. The only known photograph of this livery (which may have been a partial repaint) shows a rather 'mangled' No. 852, having received a direct hit on the cab by a bomb, whilst standing in Nine Elms shed on the night of the 15/16 April 1941. The locomotive was taken to Eastleigh and rebuilt, the work being finished in July 1942. No. 852 is now in the wartime black livery with green shaded Sunshine lettering, but has reverted to yellow serif buffer beam numerals. (RJH)

Of the two 'Lord Nelsons' in Malachite Green with BRITISH RAILWAYS in 'Sunshine'-style lettering, s854, was renumbered No. 30854 in June 1949. No. 30856 only retained the livery for two months before being repainted in Apple Green. After an overhaul in June 1949, Apple Green-liveried No. 30864 left the works with Gill sans cabside numerals and an unlettered tender. The Engine Record Card shows the tender to have been replaced by that from Malachite Green liveried No. 852 but there is conflicting information between the Engine Record Cards for Nos. 30864 and 30852, tender 1007 apparently being coupled to both locomotives between March and June 1949.

From late July 1949, all repaints were in British Railways standard Dark Green, with orange and black lining, 10in (25.4cm) cabside numerals and the first (large) British Railways totem on the tender. When the Dark Green was introduced, the red used for bufferbeams and as the backing colour of the nameplates lost the orange tint. In 1952, British Railways headquarters ruled that all nameplates should be black backed. This ruling was generally followed for main works repaints until the early 1960s, but many of the running sheds repainted the backgrounds red.

Right: No. 30858 *Lord Duncan* at Eastleigh works in 1958. No. 30858 received light casual repairs in both July and September 1958. The buffer beam has been repainted but nothing else. No. 30858 never received the second BR totem and has a water treatment yellow circle on the cabside. (CR)

Right: No. 30859 *Lord Hood* ready to leave Waterloo in August 1957. BR dark green with 8in (20.3cm) cabside numerals and the large first tender totem. (CR)

Below: No. 856 *Lord St Vincent* in postwar Malachite Green at Nine Elms in 1947, showing the 'Sunshine'-style lettering on the tender. (RKB)

Above: No. 30858 *Lord Duncan* in front of the Eastleigh shed dormitory and water tank building in May 1959. (CR)

Left: No. 857 *Lord Howe* was repainted in Malachite Green in June 1946. The livery was basically the same as that used from July 1940, using the darker shade of green but now with black-shaded 'Sunshine'-style lettering and with black backing plates to the footsteps. (IA/PRW)

Above: No. 857 *Lord Howe*, after receiving a standard boiler in March 1945. The locomotive is in the wartime black livery with green-shaded 'Sunshine'-style numerals, on a down train at Eastleigh. The cabside window is plated over and hooks for a blackout curtain can be seen on the rear edge of the cab roof. The external water gauge on the tender is apparent. (RJH)

There was some indecision initially about exactly how the lining and tender totem should be applied to the class. The widened portion of the running-plate valence was green on the first five repaints, then black on all subsequent repaints. The upper edge of the tender lining followed the whole shape of the tender side on some early repaints but subsequently ran straight across, below the turned in part. The tender totem was generally placed centrally in the lined panel but on some later repaints it was level with the cabside

Locomotive	Date	Tender lining	Totem position	Valence widening
No. 30863	August 1949	straight	low	green
No. 30865	November 1949	shaped	high	green
No. 30857	December 1949	shaped	high	green
No. 30861	March 1950	shaped	high	green
No. 30856	April 1950	shaped	high	green
No. 30853	July 1950	low	low	black

numerals. The table on page 60 shows the
arrangement on the first six repaints, the sixth
one (No. 30853) having the 'standard' layout.

The large version of the early BR totem was
used until March 1957, but No. 30857 received
a small totem in July 1952. From around 1954,
8in (20.3cm) cabside numerals were used, with the
British Railways power classification 7P above the
number. The 'Lord Nelson' class had officially been
classified 6P by British Railways until 1953, but
Eastleigh had continued to use the Western
section's A classification. Some photographs show
8in (20.3cm) cabside numerals with the A
classification. British Railways standard oval-
shaped shed plates were attached to smokebox
doors from around August 1950. These were fitted
at running sheds as well as at works, so appeared
fairly rapidly on all locomotives.

From March 1957, twelve 'Lord Nelson'
tenders received the large second BR totem. This
was applied with the heraldically incorrect right-
facing lion on the right side of the tenders until
November 1958, then with left- facing lions on
both sides subsequently. At the time of leaving
works, the four tenders which did not receive the
second totem were coupled to Nos. 30858, 30861,
30864 and 30865. A tender exchange between No.
30853 and No. 30861 in August 1959 saw No.
30853 revert to the first totem until withdrawal
whilst No. 30861 carried a right-facing second
totem on the right side of the tender until
December 1959. The locomotive then received a
General Overhaul and left-facing totems were
placed on both sides of the tender. At the time of
withdrawal, Nos. 30853, 30858, 30864 and 30865
had the first version totem on the tender.

Above: s854 *Howard of Effingham* was the first of the class to be relettered in British Railways days, March 1948. It received an s suffix to the number and BRITISH RAILWAYS tender lettering, in 'Sunshine'-style lettering. Photographed at Eastleigh, 27 March 1949. (RKB)

Left: No. 30856 *Lord St Vincent* was the only 'Lord Nelson' to be repainted with both the BR number and title in 'Sunshine'-style characters, in April 1948. To get the five figures on the cabside, 6in (15cm) numerals were used. This livery was only carried for two months, when No. 30856 was repainted in Apple Green. (IA/AA)

Right: No. 30858 *Lord Duncan* was one of two 'Lord Nelsons' to receive the 9in (23cm) 'Sunshine'-style BR numerals on the existing Southern Malachite Green livery, in June 1948. The other was No. 30859. (IA)

Right: During 1948, a number of experimental liveries were tried out on all the regions of BR. On the Southern, these included three 'Lord Nelsons' in Apple Green with red yellow and grey lining. Smoke deflectors were black and the lettering was to the Bulleid -style, but unshaded. Newly repainted No. 30864 *Sir Martin Frobisher* at Eastleigh 30 May 1948. (RKB)

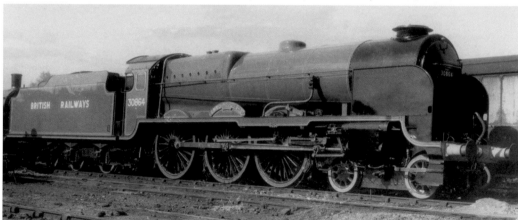

Right: In June 1949, Apple Green liveried No. 30864 *Sir Martin Frobisher* received a partial repaint, with an unlettered tender and Gill sans cabside numerals. (AEW/SWC)

Left: To run with the Apple Green painted 'Lord Nelsons', twelve carriages were repainted in a dark red and off white livery known as 'plum and spilt milk'. No. 30864 *Sir Martin Frobisher* is leaving Waterloo on the 3.30 pm to Bournemouth, 24 June 1948. The three-car Bulleid set 788 is for Weymouth, followed by six-car dining set 299 and two of the three Maunsell repainted carriages, for Bournemouth West. (IA/BR)

Left: No. 30862 *Lord Collingwood* at Eastleigh in July 1949. The locomotive was repainted in Malachite Green with Gill sans numerals and tender lettering in August 1948. (DLB)

Left: No. 30850 *Lord Nelson*, at Eastleigh, 25 March 1950, was repainted in Malachite Green with Gill sans lettering in November 1948. Then was partially repainted, with black smoke deflectors, in October 1949. The power classification A is now below the cabside numerals. (RKB)

Right: No. 30851 *Sir Francis Drake*, at Eastleigh, 15 April 1949, was repainted in Malachite Green with an unlettered tender in February 1949. It has Bulleid-type cylinders with 8in (20.3cm) piston valves and retains the short smokebox and original bogie frames. (RKB)

Right: No. 30854 *Howard of Effingham*, at Eastleigh, 12 June 1949, was repainted in Malachite Green with a blank tender in June 1949. A variant on the livery was black wheels. In April 1950 the smoke deflectors were painted black. (RKB)

Right: No. 30863 *Lord Rodney* was the first of the class to receive BR standard Dark Green livery in August 1949. The upper line on the tender lining for this first repaint is straight below the turned in side and the large first totem is centrally placed in the lined panel. No. 30863 retained Maunsell cylinders and a short smokebox. Eastleigh 21 August 1949. (RKB)

Left: No. 30856 *Lord St Vincent*, Eastleigh, 23 April 1950, was repainted in BR Dark Green in April 1950. On this locomotive and on Nos. 30857, 30861 and 30865, the tender lining followed the whole shape of the tender side. The large totem was placed level with the cabside number.
On these three locomotives (and No. 30863) the widened portion of the running plate valance was green .
(RKB)

Left: No. 30857 *Lord Howe* carried the first small tender totem from July 1952 to August 1955.
No. 30057 is on a train comprising just a Maunsell dining pair and a Bulleid three-car set.
The location looks like the New Forest, south of Lymington Junction. Possibly a Southampton to Bournemouth local is being used to move the empty dining pair to Bournemouth.
(IA/PH)

Left: No. 30852 *Sir Walter Raleigh* at Eastleigh, 7 March 1960. It received the second BR totem, with the heraldically incorrect right-facing lion on the right side of the tender. The long boiler, 860, was fitted in October 1958.
A cast iron chimney of the pattern used on the rebuilt 'Merchant Navy'-class was fitted in January 1956.
(IA/CPB)

CHAPTER FIVE

ALLOCATION & USE

The 'Lord Nelson'-class ran initially on the Eastern and
Western sections of the Southern Railway but
after World War Two all were on the Western section.

The 'Lord Nelsons' were initially allocated mainly to the Eastern sections of the Southern Railway, but with some on the Western section. Mainly used on the heaviest duties, they also appeared on other trains on the main lines. During World War Two, all were transferred to the Western section and remained there until withdrawal from service.

ALLOCATION & USE BEFORE 1940

Until World War Two, 11 or 12 'Lord Nelsons' were always based at Battersea (later known as Stewarts Lane), and were used mainly on the continental expresses from Victoria to Dover, via Tonbridge and Ashford, Maidstone and Ashford or via Chatham and Canterbury. The class was also used on normal expresses between Victoria and Ramsgate or Dover via Chatham but were not permitted to run into Charing Cross or Cannon Street which precluded use on the Kent coast expresses via Ashford. The remaining four or five locomotives were based at Nine Elms, with one briefly at Exmouth Junction in 1930. The class was used mainly on the heaviest trains on Western section of the Southern Railway, including the Atlantic Coast Express and Bournemouth Belle. After the early 1930s, the class did not work west of Salisbury. The 'Lord Nelsons' allocated to Nine Elms changed from year to year, although all

would have come onto the Western section for access to Eastleigh works. All the 'Lord Nelsons' appeared on the Eastern section, except for E860 *Lord Hood*.

Being the Southern Railway's prestige locomotives, the 'Lord Nelsons' were in demand for exhibition at special events. Although not generally used on the Waterloo to Portsmouth line, a 'Lord Nelson' was frequently on display at Portsmouth for Trafalgar Day. In August 1934, E859 *Lord Hood* was exhibited at Devonport during Navy Week. As the class were not permitted to be used on the Southern's lines west of Exeter, 'Lord Nelsons' arrived there by courtesy of the Great Western Railway (GWR), via Newton Abbot, Devon. For the Liverpool & Manchester Railway Centenary in 1930, E861 *Lord Anson* was exhibited at Liverpool carrying E850 number-plates and *Lord Nelson* nameplates. Photographs of this locomotive, taken at Eastleigh and at Liverpool, have caused confusion to locomotive historians ever since. It is reported that the real E850 ran on the Southern during this period with its own number but with *Lord Anson* nameplates but no photograph is known.

ALLOCATION & USE AFTER 1940

With the disappearance of the continental traffic at the outbreak of World War Two, the

Above: No. 30860 *Lord Hawke* near Fleet on an up boat train in 1953. An SR four-wheel luggage van and an ex-L&SWR 'Ironclad' brake 1st, lead green liveried carriages and Pullmans. (CR)

Left: No. 30859 *Lord Hood* passing Farnborough on the 10.54am Waterloo to Basingstoke in November 1959. The locomotive is carrying lamps, rather than discs, for the west of England code. (CR/GHH)

Above: E855 *Howard of Effingham* passing Folkestone Warren on the up Golden Arrow *c*1929. Behind the tender is a standard SR four-wheel luggage van and one of the six-wheel flats wagons priovided by the SE&CR to carry sealed baggage containers. (IA/FEM)

Right: No. 851 *Sir Francis Drake*, with no capuchon on the chimney, passing Bromley on the down Golden Arrow, 31 July 1937. Following declining traffic during the slump, the Golden Arrow conveyed ordinary carriages as well as Pullmans from 1932. (HCC)

Right: E859 *Lord Hood* leaving Victoria on a continental boat train *c*1930. Behind the ex-SE&CR six-wheel guards van are late SE&CR boat train carriages and a Pullman car. (IA)

Left: No. 859 *Lord Hood* passing Shorncliffe on an up boat train via Tonbridge circa 1934, the year in which the headcode was changed to that shown. (IA/ACC)

Left: Although the Eastern section 'Lord Nelsons' were primarily used on the Continental boat trains, they did work ordinary trains. No. 855 *Robert Blake*, the second of the class to have a self-trimming tender, passing Bromley on a Victoria to Ramsgate train, 20 August 1938. (HCC)

Eastern section 'Lord Nelsons' continued to be used on Victoria to Ramsgate trains. Due to unnecessary travel into Kent being seriously discouraged and with wartime loadings on the Bournemouth line increasing, all of the 'Lord Nelsons' had been transferred to the Western section by 1940. All then remained on the Western until withdrawal. Initially, all were at Nine Elms but by 1942, six were at Bournemouth, increased to 10 between 1945 and 1949. Through the 1950s, eight were at Eastleigh, three at Nine Elms and five at Bournemouth. The locomotives were used mainly on the Waterloo to Bournemouth and Weymouth express trains, with occasional visits to Salisbury and with increasing use on boat trains to and from Southampton Docks. The class also ran over the GWR route from Basingstoke to Reading and Oxford on through trains to the Midlands and North. By late 1959, all 16 of the class were at Eastleigh where the late Stephen Townroe appreciated the reliability of the class and ensured that his firemen knew how to fire them. All were withdrawn from service between 1961 and 1962.

PRESERVATION

In 1960, the British Transport Commission appointed a committee to recommend which classes of locomotives, then still in service, should be represented for a future museum collection, in addition to those locomotives already preserved. A list of 27 steam classes was produced and an example of each was retained for what later became the National Railway Museum's collection. There must have been some strong

Right: No. 30860 *Lord Hawke* passing Lyndhurst Road, July 1955 on an up express. The headcode appears to be that for a through train via Reading, with an L&SWR black centred special train disc, which was not used by the Southern. The photographer has noted that it is the Bournemouth - Birkenhead but the train formation, a Bulleid five-car set and a six-car Bournemouth dining set looks like a London train. Possible the Weymouth - Bournemouth code was not changed at Bournemouth (CR)

Right: No. 30860 *Lord Hawke* stands on the middle road at Oxford, ready to take over the 9.20 Birkenhead to Bournemouth from GWR 'Castle' 4-6-0 No. 5071 *Spitfire*, 22 August 1959. Recently overhauled, No. 5071 received a double chimney in June 1959 and rather shows up the lack of cleaning applied by Bournemouth shed to No. 30860. (CR)

Right: No. 856 *Lord St Vincent* approaching Bromley on a train to Victoria via Maidstone West, , 30 July 1938, with a mixed formation. Behind the ex-L&SWR luggage van is a six-car set consisting of en ex-L&SWR corridor brake, an L&SWR designed 'Ironclad', a Maunsell Restriction 1 carriage and three more ex-L&SWR corridor carriages. (HCC)

Left: No. 30861 *Lord Anson* on the ashpits at Nine Elms after bringing a Holland America Line boat train from Southampton in 1958. The large first totem is on the tender. (CR)

Left: No. 30861 *Lord Anson* at Eastleigh in 1957. It is in BR Dark Green with 8in (20.3cm) cabside numerals, black-backed nameplates and the first totem on the tender. (CR)

Left: Olive Green liveried No. 863 *Sir Richard Grenville*, with an experimental multiple-jet exhaust. A pair of ex-SECR 'trio' sets make a light load on a Ramsgate to Victoria train, approaching Bromley on 18 February 1939. (HCC)

Southern supporters on the committee as the list, which omitted such obvious candidates as an LNER Gresley A3, included eight Southern classes, including a 'Lord Nelson'.

No. 30850 *Lord Nelson* was claimed for the National collection and, on withdrawal, was sent to Fratton (Portsmouth) for storage, and uncoupled from the tender to fit in the roundhouse. It was when transferred to Steamtown, Carnforth (Lancashire) and restored to working order in Southern Malachite Green livery, for working special trains over the Cumbrian coast route also the Settle and Carlisle line. Knowing of the variable reputation of the 'Lord Nelson' class, many Southern supporters, including myself, were concerned that the honour of the Southern Railway was being entrusted to such a frail ambassador. To men brought up on

'Royal Scots' and 'Jubilees', the long firebox and kinked grate on the locomotive was not a problem and some excellent performances were obtained. One experienced ex-Midland region fireman commented to Stephen Townroe, who had the whole class under his care at Eastleigh by 1960, 'We treat it like a 'Royal Scot' and have no problem'.

After some years out of use, No. 30850 *Lord Nelson* was overhauled by a private group, working within Eastleigh works, then owned by Alstom. Completed during 2006, it was the last locomotive to be overhauled at Eastleigh.

The following shed allocations for the 'Lord Nelson' class are taken from the late Don Bradley's *Locomotives of the Southern Railway, Part 1* for years up to 1945 and from Ian Allan shedbooks for the years from 1950.

Left: No. 857 *Lord Howe* approaching Clapham Junction on the down Bournemouth Belle, 4 June 1933. This all-Pullman train was introduced in 1931 and was generally worked by a 'Lord Nelson' during the 1930s. The elongated headcode was used for Waterloo to Bournemouth trains from July 1928 to March 1934. (HCC)

Left: E852 *Sir Walter Raleigh* passing Vauxhall on a Waterloo to Southampton train via Alton, 16 June 1931. Until electrification at Alton in 1936, a number of Southampton trains used this route which could take the largest locomotives. The leading part of the train is an ex-L&SWR 4^{1}/$_{2}$ set, made up in the 1900s and comprising a six-wheeled van and four non-corridor bogie cariages built in the late 1890. Set trains on the Southern remained together for very long periods. (HCC)

Locomotive	1932	1937	1941	1950	1955	1960
No. 850	Battersea	Battersea	Bournemouth	Eastleigh	Eastleigh	Eastleigh
No. 851	Battersea	Battersea	Bournemouth	Eastleigh	Eastleigh	Eastleigh
No. 852	Battersea	Nine Elms	Bournemouth	Eastleigh	Eastleigh	Eastleigh
No. 853	Battersea	Battersea	Bournemouth	Eastleigh	Eastleigh	Eastleigh
No. 854	Battersea	Battersea	Bournemouth	Eastleigh	Eastleigh	Eastleigh
No. 855	Battersea	Battersea	Bournemouth	Eastleigh	Eastleigh	Eastleigh
No. 856	Battersea	Nine Elms	Nine Elms	Eastleigh	Eastleigh	Eastleigh
No. 857	Battersea	Nine Elms	Nine Elms	Eastleigh	Eastleigh	Eastleigh
No. 858	Battersea	Battersea	Nine Elms	Nine Elms	Nine Elms	Eastleigh
No. 859	Battersea	Battersea	Nine Elms	Nine Elms	Nine Elms	Eastleigh
No. 860	Nine Elms	Nine Elms	Nine Elms	Nine Elms	Nine Elms	Eastleigh
No. 861	Nine Elms	Nine Elms	Nine Elms	Bournemouth	Bournemouth	Eastleigh
No. 862	Nine Elms	Battersea	Nine Elms	Bournemouth	Bournemouth	Eastleigh
No. 863	Battersea	Battersea	Nine Elms	Bournemouth	Bournemouth	Eastleigh
No. 864	Battersea	Battersea	Nine Elms	Bournemouth	Bournemouth	Eastleigh
No. 865	Nine Elms	Battersea	Nine Elms	Bournemouth	Bournemouth	Eastleigh

Right: E852 *Sir Walter Raleigh* at Templecombe on a down stopping train. The photograph is not dated but is *c*1930 as the locomotive has smoke deflectors but the side lamp irons are still on the smokebox. Use of 'Lord Nelsons' west of Salisbury was not common. The water column indicates why the Southern bogie-type tenders needed two fillers. The bag of an L&SWR water column hung down from a fixed column, without the rotating arm provided by most other companies. (AC)

Right: No. 857 *Lord Howe*, with round-topped boiler, passing Woking on the 11.30am Waterloo to Bournemouth express, 5 April 1937. (IA/GJJ)

Right: No. 861 *Lord Anson* approaching West Weybridge (later Byfleet & New Haw) on the second portion of the 11.00 Atlantic Coast Express in August 1934. (IA/GJJ)

Above: No. 852 *Sir Walter Raleigh* passing Woking on the down Atlantic Coast Express in April 1936. (IA)

Left: No. 852 *Sir Walter Raleigh* passing Woking on the down Bournemouth Belle, during the rebuilding of the station, 4 October 1936. (IA/GJJ)

Left: No. 864 *Sir Martin Frobisher* has just passed the divergence between the west of England and Bournemouth lines at Battledown on a down Bournemouth express, the up line is on the embankment to the left. Note 9in (23cm) bufferbeam numerals indicate pre-war rather than post-war Malachite Green livery. (AC)

Right: No. 860 *Lord Hawke* approaching Winchfield on an up West of England express in 1947. Two Maunsell brake composite carriages at the front of the train are probably from Sidmouth and Exmouth, suggesting that the train is the 10.30 from Exeter. These are followed by a brand new Bulleid three-car set, with temporary ventilators above the windows as the sliding lights were delivered late. (IA/MWE)

Right: No. 30858 *Lord Duncan* passing Woking on a Waterloo to Bournemouth express, 3 September 1949. It has received the British Railways number on the existing Southern livery, retains Maunsell cylinders but has lost the snifting valves. The train appears to be a relief service. The unclassed open brake and three open 3rds at the front suggest an excursion trainset. (HCC)

Right: No. 863 *Lord Rodney* leaving Southampton Docks in 1948 on a boat train from one of the SR-owned steamers serving St Malo, Le Havre or the Channel Islands, which sailed from the Outer Dock of 1842. No. 863 was repainted Malachite Green in September 1946 and did not receive its BR number until painted in BR Dark Green in August 1949. It was the only 'Lord Nelson' never to receive Bulleid cylinders. (RKB)

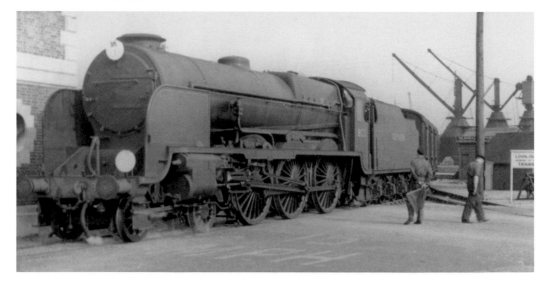

Left: No. 30854 *Howard of Effingham* passing Woking on a Waterloo to Bournemouth express, 3 September 1949. No. 30854 has recently received the BR number, replacing s854, and now has an unlettered tender. The set of SR-built Bulleid cariages has been repainted in carmine and cream. (HCC)

Left: Apple Green liveried No. 30861 *Lord Anson* approaching Farnborough on the 'plum and spilt milk' train, probably the 1.30 pm Waterloo to Bournemouth, in 1948. Three-car set 788 for Weymouth is followed by six-car dining set 299 for Bournemouth West. (AC)

Left: No. 30850 *Lord Nelson* arriving at Winchester on a Bournemouth to Waterloo train in the 1950s. The train consists of a five-car set of BR-built Bulleid carriages and a six-car dining set, all in carmine and cream. The white paint on the Upper High Street bridge is intended to make the down starter more visible to drivers of down trains, over the station canopy. (RKB/AC)

Above: No. 30861 *Lord Anson* on the ashpits at Nine Elms after bringing a Holland America line boat train from Southampton in 1958. Note the large first totem. (CR)

Right: No. 30865 *Sir John Hawkins* leaving Oxford, probably on the York to Bournemouth through train, 19 April 1950. The train consists of LNER carriages, the third and fourth are still in LNER teak livery. (RKB/AC)

Right: No. 30864 *Sir Martin Frobisher* approaching Didcot on the Bournemouth to York through train, 27 July 1950. Thompson carriages and a Gresley buffet car in carmine and cream but the leading Gresley brake is still in LNER teak livery. (IA)

Left: No. 30861 *Lord Anson*, now with the second BR totem and with AWS, leaving Eastleigh tender first on a freight for Southampton, 3 July 1961. No. 30861 is probably booked to work a boat train and has been used to take the freight, predominately vacuum fitted vans, from Eastleigh yard to Southampton. The coaling plant has deposited a good 'reserve supply' behind the bunker. (AC)

Left: No. 30862 *Lord Collingwood* approaching Basingstoke, probably on the 11.16 am Bournemouth to Newcastle, circa 1960. The Eastern Region train is now all British Railways standard carriages, except for the Gresley buffet car. All but one are in maroon livery. (JD)

Left: No. 30851 *Sir Francis Drake* passing Surbiton on a boat train from Southampton Docks, June 1955. After the Maunsell brake 3rd, the train consists mainly of British Railways standard carriages. The seventh appears to be one of Hastings line Pullman buffet cars, repainted green and used on boat trains in the late 1950s. (RKB)

Right: No. 30851 *Sir Francis Drake* at Basingstoke on a freight train from Feltham Yard (West London), 13 June 1960. (RKB/AC)

Right: No. 30850 *Lord Nelson* on a freight to Nine Elms yard (London) out of Bevois Park yard, (Southampton), in August 1956. With a higher nominal tractive effort than the 'S15' class goods 4-6-0s, and less tendency to 'slip' than the Bulleid 'Pacifics', the 'Lord Nelsons' were quite often used on freight work. (RKB)

Right: No. 30862 *Lord Collingwood* approaching Winchester Junction on a Bournemouth to Waterloo express in 1954. Despite carmine and cream having been the official livery for corridor carriages for five years, the six-car dining set at the head of the train remains in green. (RKB)

Left: No. 30864 *Sir Martin Frobisher* heading away from Lymington junction on a through train from the Western Region to Bournemouth in the late 1950s. The crest shows the leading brake composite to be in Western Region chocolate and cream, the others in a mixture of post 1956 maroon or carmine and cream. (IA)

Left: No. 30864 *Sir Martin Frobisher* leaving Bincombe tunnel on a stopping train from Bournemouth Central to Weymouth, 31 May 1950. Under the dirt, No. 30864 is in experimental Apple Green with an unlettered tender. The ex-LSWR non-corridor lavatory set, probably also in faded malachite green, is one of 37 four-car sets built between 1906 and 1910. (IA/JCF)

Left: No. 30852 *Sir Walter Raleigh* leaving Southampton Central on the 2.17pm stopping train to Bournemouth, 20 January 1956, shortly after being fitted with a cast iron chimney of the type to be fitted to the rebuilt Bulleid 'Pacifics'. Bulleid three-car set 791 retains the green livery. (IA/GW)

Right: No. 30864 *Sir Martin Frobisher* passing Battledown on the 10.54 am Waterloo to Salisbury stopping train formed of BR-built Bulleid five-car set 835. The date is 1 October but the year is not recorded. It is either 1960 or 1961 as No. 30864 has AWS but no speed recorder. (IA/DC)

Right: No. 30860 *Lord Hawke* passing Clapham Junction on the Cunarder boat train, carrying the first class passengers from either the RMS *Queen Mary* or RMS *Queen Elizabeth*. Apart from a BR standard composite at the front, the visible carriages are all Pullman Cars, of varying ages. (IA/BM)

Right: Two 'Lord Nelsons' at Waterloo, 25 March 1950. No. 30852 S*ir Walter Raleigh* is heading the 11.30 am to Bournemouth whilst '4-COR' electric unit 3113, known as 'Nelsons' due to their one-eyed appearance, is on the 11.35 am football excursion to Portsmouth. (IA/CCBH)

Above: No. 30859 *Lord Hood* leaving Alton on a diverted boat train from Southampton to Waterloo, carrying the boat train headcode and not that for Southampton - Waterloo via Alton. The original 1852 terminus station, which became the stationmaster's house when the Mid Hants Railway opened in 1865, can be seen behind the front van of the train. (IA/BK)

Left: No. 30852 *Sir Walter Raleigh* between Farnborough and Brookwood on a boat train from Southampton, 7 August 1954. The leading ex-L&SWR brake 1st had been built as a kitchen brake 1st of a boat train set in 1922. The brake 1sts remained on boat trains after the rest of the sets had been disbanded. (IA/JL)

CHAPTER SIX

NAMES

Following the Southern Railway's policy of
naming express locomotives, the new 4–6–0 class
were to be named after Naval leaders and heroes.

The Southern Railway had initiated a
policy of naming express locomotives with
the 'King Arthur' class. The new four-
cylinder 4-6-0s were named after naval heroes,
hence the 'Lord Nelson' class. The SR served the
naval bases of Chatham, Portsmouth, Portland
and Plymouth although only Chatham and
Weymouth (for Portland) would see the
'Lord Nelsons' with any regularity. The SR
occasionally arranged for one of the class to visit
Portsmouth on Trafalgar Day in pre-war years
and No. 859 *Lord Hood* was once sent to
Devonport (Plymouth), via the GWR. The
following notes on the names are taken from
the *Oxford Dictionary of National Biography*. In the
days when the differences between a King's (or
Queen's) ship, a Private ship or a Pirate ship were
somewhat indistinct, some of our heroes'
activities were questionable by latter day standards
but were accepted practice at the time.

E850 *Lord Nelson*

Horatio, Viscount Nelson (1758 - 1805). Born at
Burnham Thorpe, Norfolk, son of a clergyman.
He took part in the battle of Cape St Vincent
under Admiral Jervis (E856). He became a Rear
Admiral in 1797 and defeated a French fleet at
the Battle of the Nile in 1798, becoming Baron
Nelson of the Nile. He defeated the Danish fleet

at Copenhagen in 1802 and was appointed
Commander-in-Chief in the Mediterranean in
1805. He delivered a final defeat to the joint
French and Spanish fleets at Trafalgar in 1805 but
was shot and died during the battle.

E851 *Sir Francis Drake*

Pirate, Sea Captain and Explorer (1540 - 1596).
Born near Tavistock, Devon, he served under
Hawkins (E865) in the slave trade and commerce
raiding. Between 1577 and 1580, he sailed around
the world, on a voyage to develop trade and to
attack Spanish colonies, and was knighted in 1581.
In 1587, he entered Cadiz harbour and burned the
Spanish fleet. In 1588, Drake was second in
command to Howard (E854) in the English fleet
which defeated the Spanish Armada. He left
Plymouth for an expedition to the West Indies in
1595 and died of fever in Panama.

E852 *Sir Walter Raleigh*

Courtier, explorer and author (1554 - 1618). Born
at East Budleigh, Devon, son of the Deputy Vice
Admiral. Became a favourite of Queen Elizabeth I
and was knighted in 1585. He made a number of
unsuccessful attempts to colonise parts of North
America and fell out of favour at court. He was
implicated in a plot to assassinate King James I

Above: Nameplate of E850 *Lord Nelson*. The class leader did not have the subsidiary lettering under the nameplate. (RJH)

Left: Nameplate of No. 30856 *Lord St. Vincent*, 15 September 1960. Detail of the lining is clear, there is no lining on the firebox bands. (CR)

and was imprisoned from 1603 to 1612. In 1616, he made an unsuccessful voyage to find the mythical city of Shangri La. Raleigh was executed for treason in 1618.

E853 SIR RICHARD GRENVILLE

Naval Commander (1542 - 1591). Born at Stowe, Cornwall, son of a sea captain. Served under Hawkins (E865) in 1569, pirating in the Caribbean. Knighted circa 1575 and appointed Sheriff of Cornwall in 1576. Appointed Vice Admiral under Lord Thomas Howard (a relative of E854). In 1591 Howard's fleet of 16 ships was in the Azores when a Spanish fleet of 50 ships was reported to be approaching. Howard beat a tactical retreat but Grenville, in command of HMS *Revenge*, single-handedly attacked the Spanish fleet, with inevitable consequences.

E854 HOWARD OF EFFINGHAM

Charles Howard, second Baron Howard of Effingham (1536 - 1624). Eldest son of William Howard, the first Baron. His father had commanded the English fleet escorting King Philip II of Spain to England to marry Queen Mary in 1554 but Charles, as Lord Admiral of England, was responsible for preventing the same King Philip's Armada from landing in England 34 years later. He divided his fleet into four units

under the command of himself (E854), Drake (E851), Frobisher (E864) and Hawkins (E865). Created Earl of Nottingham in 1597, he became a diplomat.

E855 ROBERT BLAKE

Naval and Army Officer (1598 - 1657). Son of a merchant from Bridgwater, Somerset, he was elected to Parliament and supported the Parliamentarians in the Civil War. He was appointed to the Navy under the Commonwealth and took a fleet of ships to Portugal to protect British trade. He had considerable success in the Anglo-Dutch wars of 1652 to 1654. Appointed to the Mediterranean in 1654, he captured a Spanish treasure fleet in 1656. Blake died on his ship in 1657.

E856 LORD ST. VINCENT

John Jervis, Earl of St. Vincent (1735 - 1823). Son of a barrister from Stone, Staffs. He was appointed Commander of an expedition to the West Indies in 1793. Spain declared war on Britain in 1797 and Jervis, as Vice Admiral, defeated a Spanish fleet at the Battle of Cape St. Vincent. For this he was made Baron Jervis of Meaford and Earl of St. Vincent. He became first Lord of the Admiralty in 1801 and Admiral of the Fleet in 1814.

E857 *Lord Howe*

Richard Howe, Naval Officer (1726 - 1799). Born in London, second son of Viscount Howe. He succeeded his brother as Viscount Howe in 1758 and was appointed to the Board of Admiralty in 1763. He was appointed Commander-in-Chief, North America, during the American War of Independence. As Commander-in-Chief of the Channel fleet, he relieved Gibraltar from a blockade by a joint French and Spanish fleet in 1782. Howe was First Lord of the Admiralty from 1783 to 1788.

E858 *Lord Duncan*

Adam, Viscount Duncan, Naval Officer (1731 - 1804). Son of the Provost of Dundee. Appointed Commander-in-Chief North Sea fleet in 1795, he blockaded the Dutch coast with a motley assembly of elderly ships and defeated the Dutch fleet at Camperdown. He was made Baron Duncan of Lundie and Viscount Duncan of Camperdown in 1797.

E859 *Lord Hood*

Samuel Hood, first Viscount Hood (1724 - 1816). Son of the Vicar of Butleigh, Somerset. In 1781, he joined Rodney (E863) in the West Indies, prevented a French invasion of St Kitts and captured the French flagship at Saintes. Created Baron Hood of Catherington in 1782 and became Commander-in-Chief in the Mediterranean in 1793. The French fleet at Toulon surrendered to him, rather than face the revolutionary army. Created Viscount Hood of Whitley in 1796.

E860 *Lord Hawke*

Edward, First Baron Hawke (1705 - 1781). The son of a London Barrister. Appointed Rear Admiral under Anson (E861), his squadron captured three French ships at Finisterre. He introduced new ideas into naval battle tactics and was First Lord of the Admiralty in 1766 and Admiral of the Fleet in 1768. Created Baron Hawke in 1776.

E861 *Lord Anson*

George, Baron Anson (1697-1762). Son of a small landowner from Colwich, Staffs. Made a round the world journey in 1740, to capture Spanish colonies in the Pacific. Having lost most of his ships off Cape Horn, he later captured a Spanish treasure ship. Appointed Rear Admiral in 1745 and commanded the Channel squadron. Appointed to the Admiralty, he introduced reforms including formal naval ranks and uniforms. Created Baron Anson of Soberton in 1747.

Above: Nameplate of No. 30858 *Lord Duncan.* The plate is the same length as that of *Lord Howe,* but closer spaced. (AEW/SWC)

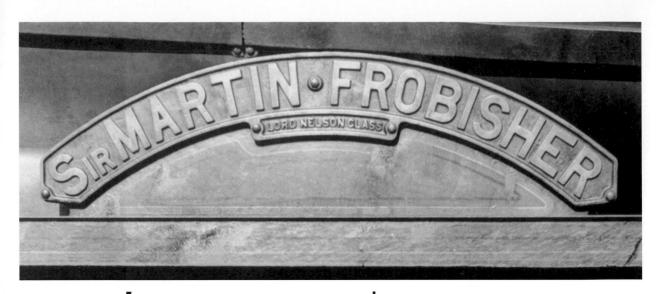

Above: Nameplate of No. 30864 *Sir Martin Frobisher*. This was one of the longest plates. Nine Elms, 10 September 1949. (AEW/SWC)

E862 *LORD COLLINGWOOD*

Cuthbert, Baron Collingwood (1748 - 1810). Son of a merchant from Newcastle upon Tyne. In 1805, he led a line of ships under Nelson (E850) at Trafalgar and took command after Nelson's death. Created Baron Collingwood of Caldbourne & Hethpoole in 1805 and appointed Commander-in-Chief Mediterranean. His health deteriorated and he died on his ship in 1810.

E863 *LORD RODNEY*

George, First Baron Rodney (1718 - 1792). Son of an Army Officer. Member of Parliament, representing a number of places. He was in the West Indies between 1779 and 1782 and was in command at the battle of the Saintes, at which nine French ships were captured. Created Baron Rodney in 1782.

E864 *SIR MARTIN FROBISHER*

Martin Frobisher (1535 - 1594). Born Altofts, Yorkshire. He made an unsuccessful voyage to find the North West Passage in 1574. Appointed Vice Admiral to Drake (E851), he took part in the defeat of the Spanish Armada in 1588, following which he was knighted. He led an expeditionary force to Brittany in 1594 and died of wounds.

E865 *SIR JOHN HAWKINS*

John Hawkins (1532 - 1595). Son of a Plymouth sea captain. He was involved in the slave trade between West Africa and America in between 1562 and 1569. Appointed Treasurer of the Navy in 1577, he encouraged the development of low-profile Galleons to replace the previous unwieldy Carracks. He took part in the action against the Spanish Armada and was knighted in 1588.

Two more recent alternative names were originally considered for E864 and E865 but were rejected.

SIR DOVETON STURDEE

Sir Frederick Charles Doveton Sturdee, First Baronet (1859 - 1925). Son of a Naval Officer from Charlton, Kent. Appointed Commander-in-Chief South Atlantic in 1914, to counter German commerce raiders. His squadron of cruisers defeated Admiral Speer's cruisers off the Falkland Islands in 1915. He was created a Baronet in 1916.

VISCOUNT JELLICOE

John, first Earl Jellicoe (1859 - 1935). Son of a Merchant Navy Captain from Southampton. Appointed to the Admiralty in 1902, he became Director of Naval Ordnance and was involved in the introduction of the 'Dreadnought' class of 'All Big Gun' battleships. He was in command of the Grand Fleet in 1916 when the German High Seas fleet put to sea, leading to the indecisive Battle of Jutland in 1916. More British ships were lost but the German fleet never put to sea in force again. He was appointed First Sea Lord in 1916 and was instrumental in developing the Convoy system to protect shipping against attack by submarines. Created Viscount Jellicoe of Scapa in 1918.

Left: No. 30856 *Lord St. Vincent* passing St Cross, south of Winchester, on the 5.23 pm Friday-only Waterloo to Bournemouth, 17 August 1962. (PHS)

Left: No. 30861 *Lord Anson* leaving Basingstoke on the 3.30 pm Waterloo to Bournemouth. On the right is No. 34030 *Watersmeet* on the 10.00 am Bradford to Poole. Both have the road, one will be held at Worting Junction. (PHS)

Left: No. 30861 *Lord Anson* passing Winchester on a boat train from Southampton, 1 September 1962. This was my last sighting of a 'Lord Nelson' in service. No. 30861 had been held at the home signal whilst No. 30936 *Cranleigh* was taking water on the preceding 11.43 am from Lymington. No. 30861 was 'chattering' well as it came through. (PHS)

Appendices: Table of Dates and Changes to Liveries and other Visible Modifications

Number Name	E 850 *Lord Nelson*	E 851 *Sir Francis Drake*	E 852 *Sir Walter Raleigh*	E 853 *Sir Richard Grenville*
Works Order No.	E124	E157	E157	E157
To Traffic	8/26	6/28	7/28	9/28
Smoke Deflectors	5/29	8/30	12/29	3/30
E-Prefix Removed	7/31	6/31	3/32	10/32
Speed Recorder	9/38	6/39	4/39	4/39
Experimental Green (1)	6/39 (g)	6/39 (f)	4/39 (e)	4/39 (d)
Experimental Green (2)	no	no	2/40 (h)	no
Standard Malachite Green (i)	3/42	1/42	no	10/40
Bulleid Black	4/44	12/43	6/42	2/43
Lemaître Exhaust	6/39	6/39	4/39	4/39
Bulleid Cylinders	3/42	6/39	3/40	2/58
Bulleid Green	11/46	11/46	3/47	6/47
BR Number & First Livery	11/48 (m1)	2/49 (n)	3/49 (n)	11/48 (m2)
Snifting Valves Removed	11/48	2/49	3/49	11/48
MN-type chimney fitted	no	no	1/56	no
Long Boiler 860 fitted	no	no	10/58	no
BR Dark Green, Large Totem	1/51	10/50	12/51	6/50
Second BR Totem	3/57 (R)	9/58 (R)	10/58 (R)	3/58 (R) (x)
Speedometer	12/60	9/60	8/60	4/60
AWS	12/60	9/60	8/60	4/60
Withdrawn	8/62	12/61	2/62	3/62
Recorded MIleage	1,349,617	1,296,946	1,249,831	not known

Bulleid Green liveries applied between 1938 and 1942
(d) Light Malachite Green with black edging and white lining
(e) Olive Green with dark green edging and yellow lining, full green smoke deflectors
(f) Light Malachite Green with dark green edging and yellow lining
(g) Light Malachite Green with black edging and yellow lining
(h) Olive Green with black edging and yellow lining
(i) Dark Malachite Green with black edging and yellow lining
British Railways Liveries at re-numbering.
(m1) Malachite Green with BRITISH RAILWAYS in Gill sans lettering. Black smoke deflectors October 1949
(m2) Malachite Green with BRITISH RAILWAYS in Gill sans lettering
(n) Malachite Green with unlettered tender

(R) Right-facing lion on right side of tender, left facing on left side. (L) Left-facing lion on both sides of tender
(x) No.30853 received a tender with the first large totem in August 1959

Below: No. 30861 *Lord Anson* leaving Buckhorn Weston tunnel, near Gillingham, on the Exeter to Salisbury leg of the Southern Counties Touring Society's special South Western Limited railtour on Sunday, 2 September 1962. (IA/GHR)

Number Name	E 854 *Howard of Effingham*	E 855 *Robert Blake*	E 856 *Lord St. Vincent*	E 857 *Lord Howe*
Works Order No.	E157	E157	E157	E157
To Traffic	10/28	11/28	12/28	12/28
Smoke Deflectors	probably 4/30	11/29	3/30	by 7/30
E-Prefix Removed	7/31	7/31	7/31	7/31
Speed Recorder	2/39	8/38	11/38	10/38
Experimental Green (1)	2/39 (c)	11/38 (a)	11/38 (a)	10/39 (g)
Experimental Green (2)	6/39 (g)	6/39 (g)	8/39 (g)	no
Standard Malachite Green (i)	5/41	12/40	7/40	9/41
Round Top Boiler fitted	no	no	no	1/37 - 6/41 1/43 - 2/45
Bulleid Black	3/45	4/43	9/42	1/43
Lemaître Exhaust	6/39	9/39 (y)	8/39 (y)	10/39
Bulleid Cylinders	11/46	12/40	7/40	10/39
Bulleid Green	11/46	6/47	7/46	6/46
BR Number & First Livery	3/48 (k1) 6/49 (n1)	2/49 (n2)	4/48 (k2) 6/48 (l)	12/49 (o)
Snifting Valves Removed	6/49	2/49	4/48	12/49
BR Dark Green, Large Totem	10/51	9/50	4/50	12/49 (q)
Long boiler 860 fitted	no	7/55 - 6/58	no	no
Second BR Totem	5/57 (R)	8/58 (R)	9/60 (L)	3/57 (R)
Speedometer	probably 7/60	6/60	9/60	7/60
AWS	10/59	6/60	9/60	7/60
Withdrawn	9/61	9/61	9/62	9/62
Recorded MIleage	not known	1.239,589	not known	not known

Bulleid Green liveries applied between 1938 and 1942
(a) Olive Green with dark green edging and yellow lining
(c) Olive Green with black edging and white lining
(g) Light Malachite Green with black edging and yellow lining
(i) Dark Malachite Green with black edging and yellow lining
British Railways liveries at re-numbering
(k1) Malachite Green with BRITISH RAILWAYS in Sunshine lettering, numbered s854.
(k2) Malachite Green with BRITISH RAILWAYS in Sunshine lettering.
(l) Apple Green with BRITISH RAILWAYS in unshaded Sunshine lettering.
(n1) Malachite green with unlettered tender and black wheels, black smoke deflectors from April 1950.
(n2) Malachite Green with unlettered tender.
(o) British Railways Dark Green with first large totem, No. 30857 had the small totem July 1952 to August 1955.

(R) Right-facing lion on right side of tender, left facing on left side. (L) Left-facing lions on both sides of tender.
(y) No. 855 and No. 856 had wide chimneys and experimental multiple blastpipes from 11/38

Left: Cylinder and valve gear detail on No. 30853 *Sir Richard Grenville* at Eastleigh 18 June 1949. (AEW/SWC)

Number Name	E 858 *Lord Duncan*	E 859 *Lord Hood*	E 860 *Lord Hawke*	E 861 *Lord Anson*
Works Order No.	E157	E157	E157	E348
To Traffic	2/29	3/29	4/29	9/29
Smoke Deflectors	probably 4/30	1/30	by 8/30	from new
E-Prefix Removed	1/32	10/31	6/33	12/32
Standard LN Boiler	yes	yes	10/36 - 8/37 (x)	yes
Speed Recorder	5/39	11/38	12/39	11/38
Experimental Green (1)	5/39 (e1)	5/39 (e2)	12/39 (g)	11/38 (a)
Experimental Green (2)	5/40 (g)	1/40 (g)	no	10/39 (g)
Standard Malachite Green (i)	5/40	none	9/40	no
Bulleid Black	9/42	5/42	10/42	8/43
Lemaître Exhaust	5/39	5/39	12/39	10/39 (y)
Bulleid Cylinders	1/51	12/46	12/39	8/43
Bulleid Green	4/46	12/46	1/47	11/47
BR Number& First Livery	6/48 (j)	2/49 (j) 6/49 (n)	11/48 (m)	5/48 (l)
Snifting Valves Removed	1/48	1/48	11/48	11/47
BR Dark Green, Large Totem	1/51	3/51	10/50	3/50
Standard LN boiler	yes	yes	3/55 - 8/62 (x)	yes
Second BR Totem	no	9/59 (L)	12/60 (L)	8/59 (R) 12/59 (L)
Speedometer	no	no	12/60	12/59
AWS	10/59	9/59	12/60	12/59
Withdrawn	8/61	12/61	8/62	10/62
Recorded Mileage	not known	not known	1.367,841	not known

Bulleid Green liveries applied between 1938 and 1942

(a)   Olive Green with dark green edging and yellow lining
(e1) Olive Green with dark green edging and yellow lining, whole green smoke deflectors
(e2) Olive Green with dark green edging and yellow lining, half green smoke deflectors
(g)   Light Malachite Green with black edging and yellow lining
(i)   Dark Malachite Green with black edging and yellow lining

British Railways liveries at re-numbering

(j)   Malachite Green with SOUTHERN tender lettering.
(l)   Apple Green with BRITISH RAILWAYS in unshaded Bulleid-style lettering.
(m)   Malachite Green with BRITISH RAILWAYS in Gill sans lettering
(n)   Malachite Green with unlettered tender, black wheels and smoke deflectors

(R)   Right-facing lion on right side of tender, Left facing on left side.
(L)   Left-facing lion on both sides of tender.
(x)   Except for these periods, No. 860 carried longer boiler 860.
(y)   861 had a wide chimney and experimental multiple blastpipe from November 1938

Right: Motion on preserved No. 850 *Lord Nelson* at Liverpool Road station, Manchester, 9 August 1980. (PHS)

Number Name	E 862 Lord Collingwood	E 863 Lord Rodney	E 864 Sir Martin Frobisher	E 865 Sir John Hawkins
Works Order No.	E348	E348	E348	E348
To Traffic	10/29	10/29	11/29	11/29
E-Prefix Removed	2/32	6/32	12/31	6/32
Crank Setting Changed	no	no	no	12/33
Double Kylchap chimney	8/34 - 5/39	none	no	6/38 - 6/39
Speed Recorder	10/38	11/38	11/38	6/39
Experimental Green (1)	5/39 (f)	11/38 (a)	1/39 (b)	6/39 (g)
Experimental Green (2)	4/40 (g)	6/39 (f)	6/39 (g)	no
Standard Malachite Green (i)	no	12/40	4/41	9/40
Bulleid Black	7/43	11/42	6/43	5/43
Lemaître Exhaust	5/39	6/39 (y)	6/39 (z)	6/39
Bulleid Cylinders	4/40	no	5/48	9/40
Bulleid Green	8/48	9/46	1/47	6/46
BR Number& First Livery	8/48 (m)	8/49 (o)	5/48 (l)	8/48 (m)
Snifting Valves Removed	8/48	11/47	5/48	8/48
BR Dark Green, Large Totem	12/50	8/49	4/51	11/49
Second BR Totem	6/58 (R)	10/57 (R)	no	no
Speedometer	5/61	no	no	no
AWS	5/61	10/59	10/59	no
Withdrawn	10/62	2/62	1/62	5/61
Recorded MIleage	1,311,443	not known	not known	not known

Bulleid Green liveries applied between 1938 and 1942
(a)   Olive Green with dark green edging and yellow lining
(b)   Maunsell Green with black edging and white lining
(e)   Olive Green with dark green edging and yellow lining
(f)   Light Malachite Green with dark green edging and yellow lining
(g)   Light Malachite Green with black edging and yellow lining
(i)   Dark Malachite Green with black edging and yellow lining

British Railways liveries at re-numbering
(l)   Apple Green with BRITISH RAILWAYS in unshaded Bulleid-style lettering.
(m)   Malachite Green with BRITISH RAILWAYS in Gill sans lettering
(o)   British Railways Dark Green with large first totem

(R)   Right-facing lion on right side of tender, left facing on left side.

(y)   No. 863 had a wide chimney with a single blastpipe from June 1938, experimental multiple blastpipe from November 1938
(z)   No. 864 had a wide chimney and experimental multiple blastpipe from January 1939

Below: Preserved No. 850 *Lord Nelson* on the Settle to Carlisle line in the 1980s. The 'Lord Nelsons'' 'achilles heel', the long firebox with a kinked grate, vanished when No.850 arrived at Steamtown, Carnforth. A fireman told Stephen Townroe 'We treat it like a Royal Scot and have no problem'. (CR)

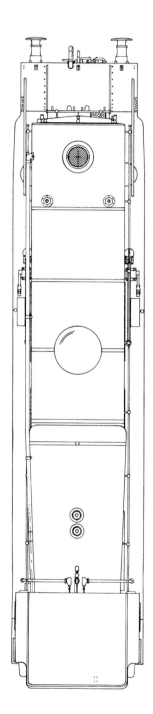
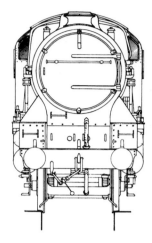
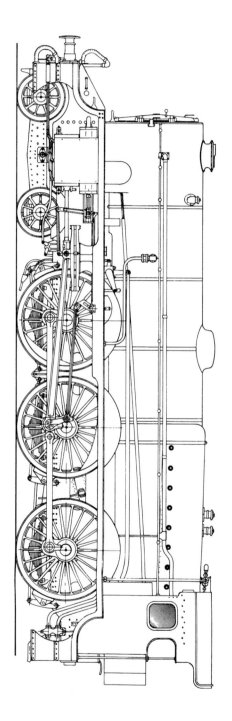

Maunsell 4-6-0 Lord Nelson class

© Copyright 2007 *Railway Modeller*/Ian Beattie

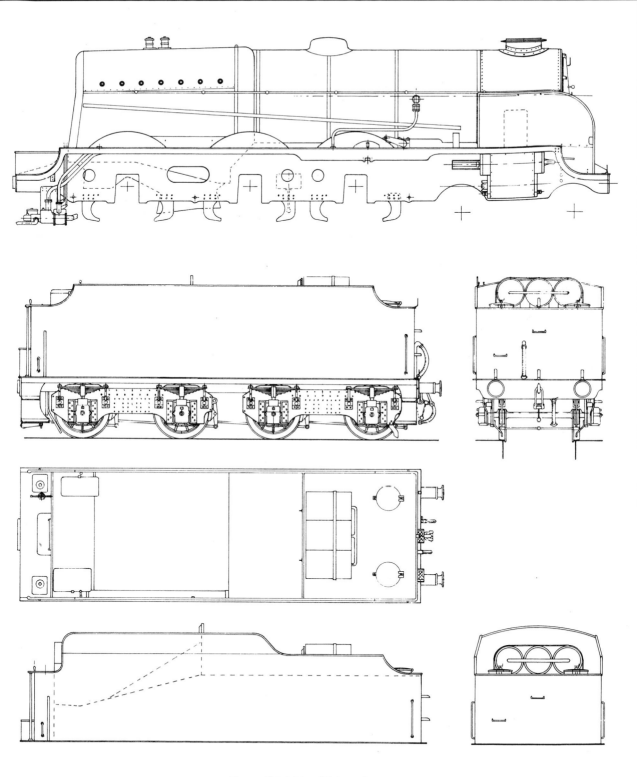

Maunsell 4-6-0 Lord Nelson class

© Copyright 2007 *Railway Modeller*/Ian Beattie

Above: No. 30862 *Lord Collingwood* waits at Medstead & Four Marks, on the Winchester to Alton line, with a troop train. (CR/ST)